This book is available at a special discount when ordered in bulk quantities. For information contact Special Sales Department, AMACOM, an imprint of AMA Publications, a division of American Management Association, 1601 Broadway, New York, NY 10019

Printing number

10 9 8 7 6 5 4 3 2 1

Contents

Introduction

Mergers and acquisitions (M&A) occur when two or more organizations join together all or part of their operations. The differences between mergers and acquisitions relate mainly to

- the relative size of the individual companies in the business combination
- ownership of the combined business
- management control of the combined business.

Mergers

Mergers can be defined in broad as well as narrow terms.

In its broadest definition, a merger can refer to any takeover of one company by another, when the businesses of each company are brought together as one.

A more narrow definition is the coming together of two companies of roughly equal size, pooling their resources into a single business. The stockholders or owners of both pre-merger companies have a share in the ownership of the merged business and the top management of both companies continues to hold senior management positions after the merger. An acquisition, in contrast, is the takeover of the ownership and management control of one company by another. Control is the key test of the distinction between a merger and an acquisition.

A narrow definition of merger, as distinct from an acquisition, has also been developed. A merger exists when

- neither company is portrayed as the acquirer or the acquired
- both parties participate in establishing the management structure of the combined business
- both companies are sufficiently similar in size that one does not dominate the other when combined
- all or most of the consideration involves a share swap rather than a cash payment, etc. In a merger, very little if any cash changes hands.

Example 1

In September 1992 Reed International and Dutch publisher Elsevier announced plans to merge without any money changing hands. The $5.2 billion merger created the world's third largest publishing group. The parent company is 50:50 owned by Reed International and Elsevier, and these companies have retained their separate stock market listings on the London and Amsterdam stock markets. In recognition of its larger size at the time of the merger, Reed also obtained about 11% of Elsevier's equity. In 1997, Reed Elsevier agreed, subject to regulatory approval, a further merger with Dutch publishers Wolters Kluwer that would have resulted in a group with combined sales of around Fl15 billion, with once again an Anglo-Dutch holding company structure. In the event the merger did not proceed.

Example 2

In January 1998, the two largest UK pharmaceutical companies, SmithKline Beecham and Glaxo Wellcome announced their plans to merge. This deal, that was subsequently abandoned, was worth more than £100 billion and would have created the biggest drugs company in the UK, and the third biggest company in the world. The move followed a series of mergers in the industry over the previous five years that was driven in the main by opportunities for cost-cutting by combining research and development facilities.

Acquisitions

An acquisition, or takeover, occurs when one company acquires from another company either

- a controlling interest in the company's stocks, or
- a business operation and its assets.

The purchase consideration could take the form of stocks in the acquiring company. Stockholders in the company that is taken over exchange their stocks for stocks in the acquiring company, thus becoming minority stockholders in the enlarged company post-acquisition. Often, however, the purchase consideration for an acquisition is paid largely or entirely in cash.

Example
Gamma Inc. has assets of $20 million and liabilities of $5 million. Delta plc wishes to acquire Gamma's business.

Analysis
Delta could offer to take over Gamma by purchasing its share capital. Alternatively, Delta could offer to buy Gamma's assets, leaving Gamma's management to settle the company's liabilities out of the overall purchase consideration.

The method of acquisition, buying the company or buying its assets, could be a matter for negotiation. By purchasing a company, the buyer acquires its liabilities as well as its assets; the buyer also acquires any tax losses that the purchased company might have accumulated to set off against future profits.

Full and Partial Acquisitions

Acquisitions of companies can be either full or partial. In a full acquisition, the acquirer buys all the stock capital of the purchased company. In a partial acquisition, the acquirer obtains a controlling interest, normally over 50% of the equity stocks, but less than 100%.

Partial acquisitions could occur

- by agreement, when stockholders in the target company want to retain a stake in the company postacquisition
- because some stockholders in the target company refuse to sell their stocks.

In takeover negotiations, rival bidders can structure deals in significantly different ways. One bidder might want to buy the entire target company. Another might propose to buy a majority stake, leaving the seller with a minority interest.

Example

Brent Walker, the UK pubs, betting and property group, was forced to seek refinancing from its banks when it ran into financial difficulties. One part of the Brent Walker group, the William Hill betting shops subsidiary, was ring-fenced from the rest of Brent Walker, and had its own syndicate of banks that were owed about £350 million ($480million). This loan was due to mature on March 1, 1994.

William Hill was put up for sale. One consortium of bidders, assembled by a merchant bank, made a £360 million bid for the entire company, subject to the bid not being regarded as hostile by Brent Walker's board of directors.

It was reported that at least one other bid had been received, involving an offer to buy a majority stake in William Hill, leaving Brent Walker with a minority stake. It was thought that the management of Brent Walker would prefer to retain an equity stake in William Hill, so that any rise in the subsidiary's value would benefit its own creditors.

Another rumor was the possibility that Brent Walker might ask the William Hill consortium banks to refinance the subsidiary's loan until Brent Walker's stocks could be floated on the stock market. A flotation might have valued the company at around £500 million, allowing Brent Walker to sell a majority stake in the flotation, repay the William Hill banks and still retain a substantial equity stake in William Hill.

William Hill eventually was sold in late 1997 to Nomura International plc for £700 million, with the proceeds used to reduce Brent Walker's debt, by then at £1.3 billion.

Joint Ventures

A joint venture is a business partnership in which two or more companies agree to invest cash or other assets in a particular project or business activity. The partners can establish a separate company in which they hold stocks in proportion to their investment in the venture. However they do not generally purchase or exchange each other's stocks, and the main purpose of many joint ventures is to create a strategic alliance between separate companies with common interests and complementary skills or experience. In these respects, joint ventures differ from mergers and acquisitions.

M&A Activity

An increasing proportion of M&A activity now involves cross-border deals and companies outside the Anglo Saxon countries where mergers and acquisitions have a longer history. For example, during 1997 approximately 75 cross-border transactions with a value of over $1 billion each were agreed.

The main reason for the growing number of cross-border takeovers, mergers and joint ventures is the desire to compete, or survive, in new world markets.

- Large consumer and industrial markets are developing in several parts of the world, in particular in the Asia Pacific region and in Latin America.
- Recently large areas of the world have been opened up to commercial exploitation, notably the former communist bloc countries.
- Trade barriers have been removed in some areas, notably the European Union (EU), making access to foreign markets easier.
- Many product markets have become international. Improvements in worldwide communications have made it easier for management to control businesses in other countries.
- Privatization in eastern Europe in the early 1990s and more recently in Latin America has created new investment opportunities.
- A disparity in valuations of similar companies in different countries can create opportunities for takeovers at an attractive price.
- Succession problems in continental Europe, particularly in France and Germany, have led to a willingness to contemplate a deal with a foreign purchaser.

Reasons for Buying

Reasons for wanting to acquire other companies include

- pursuing a growth strategy
- defensive reasons
- financial opportunities.

Many companies use acquisitions to pursue a strategy for growth in turnover, market share and profits. Strategic reasons for acquisitions are the subject of Chapter 2.

In some takeovers, the buyer acquires more businesses than it wants to keep. In such circumstances it will try to sell off unwanted businesses, retaining only those that fit its strategic objectives.

Defensive reasons for acquisitions include the need for reorganization within an industry: and a merger or acquisition can help to eliminate over-capacity.

Financial opportunities occasionally can encourage mergers or acquisitions. One of the reasons for the agreed merger in 1993 between chemicals group Akzo of the Netherlands and Nobel of Sweden was the opportunity it gave Nobel to refinance its heavy debts at a much lower interest cost. As another example, a buyer may wish to make use of tax losses available in a target company.

A distinction can be made between

- companies that seek acquisitions to add value to their business by achieving a better rate of growth, and
- companies that identify takeover targets where they can capture and exploit the value that already exists in the business, without necessarily creating more growth.

Corporate Raiders

Companies can make a distinction between acquisitions for commercial or strategic reasons, and acquisitions for investment management reasons. Corporate raiders primarily are concerned with the potential financial benefits of takeovers. They look for undervalued companies to buy cheaply, and unlock the value quickly, perhaps by breaking up the acquired company into smaller divisions that can be resold at a profit.

Reasons for Selling

A company might be willing to sell some of its businesses. The reasons for selling could be

- to raise money, perhaps to pay off debts or to raise cash for future acquisitions
- an attractive offer price
- the desire to sell off an unprofitable part of the business
- a wish to sell off non-core activities that do not fit commercially or strategically with the rest of the seller's businesses

- when a business can realize greater value to stockholders by being sold rather than retained
- a lack of funds to invest in developing the business, and a consequent willingness to sell to a buyer willing to invest the funds the business needs.

A company that runs into financial difficulties and has to seek refinancing from its banks could be forced to agree, as a condition of the refinancing, to sell off businesses to raise cash for repaying some of the loans.

National and state authorities have sold businesses to private sector buyers, i.e. authorities privatize their operations to raise cash, and often become a customer of the privatized company.

Example
Between 1992 and 1996, the Russian government privatized its oil industry, dividing it into 16 parts that were then sold to institutional and financial investors. In some cases, investors made loans to the Russian government, receiving stocks in the privatized business in exchange. More recently the sector has moved towards reconsolidation through mergers of the privatized companies.

Conclusion

In the following chapters a range of issues will be considered. These will include the strategic reasons for mergers and acquisitions, the price and purchase consideration or merger terms, the process of investigating and making a takeover bid, defenses against hostile bids and regulatory restrictions on mergers and acquisitions.

M&A Strategies

Mergers and acquisitions can be categorized into two groups

- financial acquisitions, where the buyer is driven primarily by financing considerations, and
- strategic mergers and acquisitions, where the buyer is driven primarily by commercial considerations.

The thinking behind each type of acquisition is different. Financial acquisitions are often opportunistic deals that do not fit into any broad plan for developing the business. This chapter concentrates mainly on strategic mergers and acquisitions.

Strategic Approach to Acquisitions

Acquisition-based growth and organic growth should be twin platforms of a large company's strategic approach to developing its business. In addition, companies needing to concentrate their resources on core activities in growing industries should consider a strategy for divestment of non-core activities.

A strategic approach requires

- identifying corporate objectives
- developing strategies to achieve those objectives, and deciding between acquisitions and organic development as the more appropriate option in each case

- selecting candidates for acquisition. This calls for an evaluation of potential candidates in terms of cost savings, profit enhancement, other synergies and long-term strategic benefits
- deciding the value of the acquisition and making a bid
- making the acquisition.

Corporate Objectives and Mission Statements

A company's primary corporate objective is probably a financial one. This objective could be expressed in general terms, as seeking to maximize or increase shareholder value. The objective could be more specific; for example to increase earnings per share every year or to achieve a return on capital employed in excess of a stated target.

A company also can have a mission statement in which it sets out the basic principles it will follow to achieve its objectives. It could have a mission, for example, to provide transport, supply energy or provide a retailing service to consumers.

Companies should have business objectives that support their primary financial objective. Business objectives include

- market leadership in the form of geographical market leadership, within a country, a group of countries or globally
- technological leadership
- providing a high quality product or service, for example, the quality of water provided by water supply companies
- innovation
- being the lowest cost producer in the industry.

There could be financial policy constraints on business objectives. For example, a company might have the objective of avoiding excessive financial risks. As a consequence, it might decide to limit its borrowings (gearing). This could affect its plans for expansion.

Strategy and Objectives

A strategy is a broad formula for how an organization intends to achieve its objectives. Objectives alone do not give a company any sense of direction or scope. Strategy establishes the rules or guidelines and specific steps on how objectives should be achieved. Product/market strategies, for example, create a framework for decisionmaking by indicating how the company intends to compete in its markets, and what its goals should be for each of its products and markets.

Examples of product/market strategy are

- to increase market share in order to achieve economies of scale and better profit margins
- to obtain lower cost production facilities
- to diversify into new markets, because existing markets are not large enough to support future growth
- to diversify into new products or services, because the company's existing product range is in decline or is insufficient to sustain future growth.

Acquisitions and Organic Growth

Acquisitions can be the best method of achieving strategic aims. At other times, organic development – in-house development – is more appropriate. The choice between acquisition and organic growth for new product/market developments depends on a number of key factors.

Factor	Acquisition-based strategy	Organic growth strategy
Timescale	Necessary for short-term results and immediate market presence	Probably more appropriate for a long-term strategy to develop a market position
Cost	Acquisitions are often expensive	Costs are difficult to quantify. If successful, costs

		can be much lower than with acquisition-led growth
Barriers to entry	Acquisitions appropriate where existing competition is strong, thus making a "start up" entry to the market difficult to achieve	Organic growth appropriate where legislation and regulations prevent a company from buying market share
Business risks	Usually known, from the track record of target companies pre-acquisition. A major unsuccessful acquisition can spell disaster	Risks high. However, losses can be limited by pulling out if things go wrong
Stage of market development	Acquisitions best suited to a mature market, or to buy in established expertise/know how in a young market	Organic growth often well suited to a young market. Growth occurs as the market develops

Synergy

In mergers and takeovers, synergy is the additional benefit that can be derived from combining the resources of the bidding and target companies. When synergy exists, the total returns from the combined organization exceed the total returns of the two companies before the merger or acquisition. Synergy has been described as the 2 + 2 = 5 effect.

Synergy can be an essential part of the financial success of a merger or acquisition. The chairman of Dutch chemicals group Akzo commented on the merger of his company with Nobel of Sweden that was announced in November 1993, "There are plenty of opportunities for the chemicals operations to prove that the sum of one plus one is more than two".

However, synergy does not always occur in a merger or acquisition, and all too often, hoped-for synergies fail to materialize.

In his book *Corporate Strategy*, Igor Ansoff classified different types of synergy as

- *sales synergy*. This occurs where a merged organization can benefit from common distribution channels, sales administration, advertising, sales promotion and warehousing.
- *operating synergy*. This can arise from a better utilization of facilities and personnel, and bulk-order purchasing to reduce materials costs.
- *investment synergy*. This can arise from the joint use of plant and equipment, joint research and development efforts, and having common raw materials inventories.
- *management synergy*. This can arise when the top management of one of the companies uses their relevant experience, after the merger or acquisition, to resolve the problems of the other company. In other words, a management team can bring its skills and experience to bear on the other company, and so help to improve its performance.

Often the term synergy is used to mean cost savings and has been associated with redundancies and closures following an acquisition.

In many cases acquisition also can have financial benefits for the purchaser that include

- enhanced asset backing for the bidder's shares where the bidder has a lower ratio of net assets to share value than the target company
- higher earnings per share depending, however, on the profits of the acquired company and the purchase price
- improved earnings quality (consistency of annual profits)
- greater and cheaper access to better cash flows and liquidity, or to financing sources.

Aggressive and Defensive Strategies

Mergers and acquisitions can be the outcome of either an aggressive or a defensive strategy.

By using an aggressive strategy, a company will seek to improve its market position. Mergers and acquisitions are intended to create a bigger company with larger markets for its products, and with the resources to produce on a bigger scale and more cheaply through economies of scale. Target companies for takeover bids are commonly existing competitors, or similar companies operating in different markets.

Mergers and acquisitions are common in industries and markets that are in the process of becoming more global. Major suppliers to growing markets need to expand in order to remain competitive.

Often defensive mergers and acquisitions are made in order to survive in a changing industry. A major acquisition by one company prompts a similar response from others. Recently, the number of major competitors in many industries, ranging from accountancy to pharmaceuticals, has shrunk because of mergers, acquisitions and strategic alliances. At the same time, their markets have become more international.

Example
In the US communications industry there has been substantial consolidation in recent years. Since the passing of the 1996 Telecommunications Act that deregulated TV, radio and telephone businesses, the structure of this sector has changed dramatically. Between 1996 and the beginning of 1998, more than 4,000 of the 10,000 US radio stations changed hands in response to new opportunities for growth.

Acquisitions in one industry can be prompted by M & A activity or market changes in the industries of suppliers or customers. For example, in January 1998, Security Capital Industrial Trust, the US transport and distribution company, bought ASG, the Swedish transport company. This acquisition was prompted by the need to offer an integrated, international distribution and logistics service to SCIT's major international clients.

A further motive for a takeover or merger could be to eliminate over-capacity in a market by removing a competitor.

Example

In the European steel industry, serious over-capacity in Germany prompted the 1997 DM13.6 million hostile takeover bid by Krupp Hoesch for its rival Thyssen. The bid was eventually dropped, and the two companies instead entered discussions on a joint venture for their steel interests.

Strategies for Growth

M&A strategy is based on a growth objective. An acquisition strategy for growth can seek to develop products and markets in any of four ways

- by market penetration, including cross-border acquisitions
- by horizontal diversification
- by vertical integration
- by conglomerate diversification.

Market Penetration

Market penetration means developing new and larger markets for a company's existing products.

A market penetration strategy often will be pursued within markets that are becoming more international or global. Cross-border mergers and acquisitions can be a means of becoming, or remaining, a major player in such markets.

Example

Quebecor Printing, Canada's largest printer and north America's second largest, acquired printing businesses in France and the UK in the mid-1990s, as part of a pan-European expansion strategy. On announcing the next stage of his strategy in late 1997, with the £188 million hostile bid for Watmoughs, chairman Charles Cavell said, "I'm going to expand here. It's that simple". Quebecor was then outbid by

Bahrain-based Investcorp through its printing vehicle Webinvest that was pursuing a strategy of buying and rationalizing UK printers.

In manufacturing industries, some multinational companies have pursued a policy of establishing production facilities in different parts of the world, either by setting up factories on a greenfield site or by purchasing an existing production company. The motives for diversifying production into other countries could be to benefit from cheaper labor costs, or to deal with the threat of tariff or other import barriers. For example, the UK labor market is less regulated and less unionized than in France or Germany, a factor taken into account by Quebecor in its bid for Watmoughs.

Horizontal Diversification

When a company grows through horizontal diversification, it expands into markets for products that it has not made before, but which are similar to its existing product range. The company expects to use its existing resources including distribution channels, marketing skills or management skills etc., to improve the performance of acquired companies with whose business they are roughly familiar. For example, a goldmining company could acquire a copper mine, and hope to use its mining and engineering management skills and commodity markets knowledge, to run the new business. A tobacco company might take over a food producer and use common distribution channels. This was a factor in the acquisition of Kraft and General Foods by Philip Morris, the tobacco company.

An acquisition strategy based on horizontal diversification rarely focuses on one or two specific targets. More usually, companies take a view of the business or businesses they wish to be in, and consider any potential targets that might emerge.

If a company pursues a strategy for growth through horizontal diversification, it is not necessarily seeking a dominant market position. It might simply keep looking out for potential targets in a focused sector of an industry.

Example

In late 1997 the luxury UK motor company, Rolls-Royce Motor Cars, was put up for sale by its parent company Vickers. It soon became a target for a number of trade purchasers, including German manufacturers Mercedes-Benz, BMW and Volkswagen. These companies had identified Rolls-Royce as a means of expanding within their own industry, but in a different geographical area.

Horizontal diversification can be a fairly high-risk measure for obtaining a strategic position in newly emerging markets when there is doubt about whether the product or the market will ever develop sufficiently. A major example of horizontal diversification risk in recent years has been in the media industry, with the development of new media products such as satellite and subscription television.

Vertical Integration

Vertical integration is the combination of a company's business with the business of a supplier or of a customer.

- A gas supply company might take over or merge with its own supplier, a gas exploration and development company. Equally, a manufacturer of computers might seek to purchase a producer of microchips. These are examples of backwards or upstream vertical integration, where a company seeks to grow by acquiring a supplier company further up the industry's supply chain.
- A holiday tour operator might acquire a chain of travel agents, and use the travel agents to promote its own holidays rather than those of rival tour operators. This is an example of forward or downstream vertical integration, involving the takeover of a customer's business.

However, in many industries there is a continuing move away from vertical integration and towards decentralization and sub-contracting. For example, Ford at one time manufactured cars through all stages of production, from iron ore to completed car, at its Rouge plant. Reliance on in-house components has been reduced during the past 20 years or so in the face of severe competition from lower-cost Japanese producers.

Vertical integration is usually motivated by a wish

- to secure a source of supply for key materials or services
- to secure a distribution outlet or a major customer for the company's products
- to improve profitability by expanding into the high-margin activities of suppliers or customers.

Example 1

In early 1998 Compaq Computer Corporation, the largest PC maker in the world, acquired Digital Equipment Corporation for $9 billion. DEC's high-end Alpha-chip technology and servers fitted neatly into Compaq's existing products, while its support services division was viewed as another valuable addition. Following the acquisition, Compaq has become a complete computer services company.

Example 2

Between 1996 and 1998 there was a series of bids for UK regional electricity companies by UK and overseas power generators. In 1997 The Energy Group plc took over Eastern Group plc, the largest regional electricity company (REC) in the UK, in a deal that obtained UK regulatory approval. And in 1998 The Energy Group was in turn taken over by Texas Utilities that won the bidding battle in contest with rival bidder PacifiCorp. Texas was able to achieve geographical, vertical and horizontal integration through this acquisition.

Conglomerate Diversification

Conglomerates are groups of companies that operate in widely diverse industries. At one time it was generally believed that conglomerates had a low investment risk for shareholders, compared with companies that concentrated their activities in a single industry. In a conglomerate, risk is lower because successful performers balance badly performing subsidiaries in the group, and the annual profits of the conglomerate as a whole should be fairly predictable.

This view is no longer widely accepted. It is argued that if investors wish to reduce their risk by diversifying, they can choose which industries to invest in, and build up their own investment portfolio of shares in companies in those industries. As markets grow, companies often can achieve the best returns for shareholders by concentrating their resources and skills on core business activities. Consequently, many companies have sold off non-core businesses, and the trend in strategic planning has been away from conglomerate diversification and towards product/market specialization.

Even so, there are some companies that continue a strategy of conglomerate diversification, believing they can identify companies as takeover targets, and improve their performance post-acquisition. Target companies can be in any industry. The skills of the conglomerate lie in identifying takeover targets, buying them at a low price, sorting out their problems and unlocking the value that exists in their businesses. After the successful turnaround, the subsidiaries either can be sold off at a profit, or retained as operating subsidiaries.

Two highly successful conglomerates have been Hanson and Tomkins. The success of both has in part been due to a decision to seek acquisitions in the US. Tomkins established its US presence by acquiring Smith & Wesson in 1987 for $113 million, Murray Ohio in 1988 for $228 million, and Philips Industries in 1990 for $550 million. In December 1992, Tomkins also acquired Rank Hovis McDougall, the milling and baking group. Since then a number of smaller acquisitions and disposals have followed, in line with its strategy, reiterated in late 1997, of focusing the group on the development of a number of strategic business activities with potential for long-term growth.

Successful conglomerates are noted for their ability to identify takeover targets and not pay too much for them. The purchase consideration also can be arranged to limit the financial risks of an acquisition. When the potential commercial risk is high, the financial risk should be kept low.

However, during the late 1990s there has been a trend away from conglomeration, with Hanson de-merging and Tomkins re-focusing on key activities.

Success or Failure of Strategic Acquisitions

A strategy based on acquisitions does not always work. In the short term, operating costs can be higher than anticipated, or the benefits much lower. When expected synergies do not occur, and the acquired company has a disappointing performance, the cost of the acquisition, in the short term at least, can be excessive. The financial performance of the group as a whole can be seriously damaged.

Overseas acquisitions in particular can be high-risk ventures. Problems of management control inevitably occur, and the hoped-for synergy often fails to materialize. There have been many instances of disappointing performance by the acquired subsidiary, at least in the short term.

In the long term, an unsuccessful strategy might be abandoned and replaced by a completely different one, often partly as a result of appointing a new chief executive or chairman with a different vision of what the company should be doing.

Example
Between 1980 and 1985, Guinness plc focused on three main areas of activity: drinks, retailing, and health. The company pursued an acquisition-based strategy to develop these businesses. In 1985, the company moved into the market for spirits, with the acquisition in a hostile takeover bid of Arthur Bell. It then made a controversial hostile bid for United Distillers.

With the appointment of a new chief executive in 1987, Guinness reassessed its strategy and decided to focus on its drinks business. In 1987, Guinness and French drinks and luxury goods manufacturer LVMH entered into a joint arrangement to distribute their respective drinks in key foreign markets. Subsequently the companies built up a 24% stake in each other.

This focus resulted in the 1997 merger of Guinness with rival spirits and leisure company, Grand Metropolitan, to form Diego plc, the world's largest spirits company.

Strategic Mergers

The strategy behind business combinations of roughly equal partners is often based on the recognition that the separate companies are not big enough to achieve a predominant position in world markets on their own, even through acquisitions. Joining together with another company of comparable size therefore is an alternative to an acquisition strategy.

The merger of direct competitors could have the effect of simply knocking one rival company out of the market, leaving all the remaining companies to improve their market share. It does not follow for example that if two companies, each holding a 20% market share agree to merge, their total market share after the merger will be 40%. If the merged company can achieve synergies, and reduce its costs and prices, or improve the quality of its product or service, its market share could exceed 40%. On the other hand, other competitors in the market could benefit from the merging of two rivals to increase their own market share, and the merged company could have less than 40% of the market.

In a merger, two companies can bring together similar but largely complementary products and services.

In a merger within a high technology industry, companies may benefit from a pooling of research and development costs, so that R&D resources could be utilized more effectively. This was a factor in the attempted merger in early 1998 between SmithKline Beecham and Glaxo Wellcome in the pharmaceuticals industry.

The Takeover Process

The process of acquiring a company starts with a search for potential acquisition candidates. An initial valuation is needed when a target has been identified, so that an indicative price, or even a firm price, can be determined. In a negotiated takeover, discussions will take place and further investigations will be carried out to reassess the valuation. A price and purchase consideration is then agreed with the targeted company's management or major shareholders. Where necessary, the regulatory authorities must be advised of the bid and consulted about the acceptability of its terms.

This chapter deals with the process of searching for takeover targets, identifying them and negotiating a takeover deal. Valuations, the purchase consideration, dealing with the regulatory authorities and hostile bids are dealt with in later chapters.

Role of Advisers

Both the bidding company and the target company in a takeover will obtain assistance from their bank, an investment bank, attorneys, reporting accountants, and for companies with a stock market listing, their registrars. International attorneys must be consulted in a cross-border takeover. The banks of each company also could appoint solicitors to represent their interests.

Investment banks primarily are involved in the financial aspects of takeovers, advising clients on price, purchase consideration, regulatory measures, stock market procedures in the event of a hostile bid, as well as raising finance. The strategic and commercial aspects, identifying targets and assessing their potential value, are commonly dealt with by the company's own management, but can be assigned to outside consultants, including banks, especially in other countries. Advisers will help both the bidder and the target company in hostile takeovers to formulate offer documents or defense documents.

The role of advisers can be to give independent financial advice to shareholders. The stockholders of the target company should receive advice about the suitability of the offer. Stockholders of the company making the bid need advice when their approval for a bid is required.

The Takeover Process

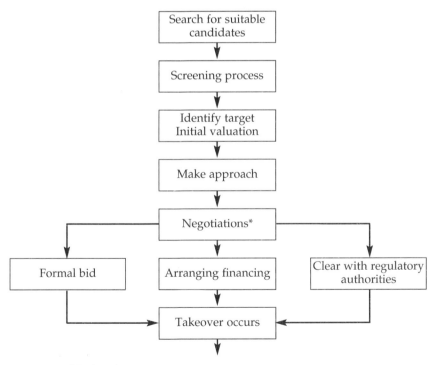

*Negotiated bids only

Searching for Acquisition Candidates

In many cases, the potential target for an acquisition is a company that is well known to the bidder. A company could, however, appoint an individual or team to search for potential acquisitions.

Information about possible candidates can come from various sources. More than one source should be used to build up a profile of each potential target.

Initially, publicly available information can be used to identify companies operating in targeted industries or geographical markets. Directories provide information about companies operating within each industry. They are published by various organizations, including trade associations and information professionals. The most suitable depends on the type of acquisition being sought. On-line electronic databases also can be used.

Further information regarding potential takeover candidates should be gathered and studied. Information sources include

- stock market analyst reports for listed public companies
- trade journals and publications
- trade associations
- business literature and on-line search facilities
- stockholder lists
- research studies
- contacts in the business, or other contacts with knowledge of the potential target, for example investment banks
- published financial accounts
- the company's own publicity brochures or product literature, including its website.

Screening Process

When there are several potential acquisition candidates in the same industry and market, there should be a screening process to rank the candidates in order of desirability, and to eliminate candidates that do not meet all requirements.

The screening process could be divided into two stages

- eliminating candidates that are unlikely to meet predetermined strategic requirements
- a financial evaluation and ranking of the remaining candidates.

In the first stage of screening, the criteria for selection will include

- size: some companies will be too big to buy and others will be too small to consider
- geographical area: some companies will sell in markets that are too wide, not wide enough, or located in unsuitable countries or regions of the world
- product mix: some companies will have a product mix that is too broad, or too narrow.

Candidates can be ranked by market share and product/market mix.

The purpose of this analysis is to identify candidates that are worth considering, with respect to size, markets and product mix. Candidates for takeover often will sell products or operate in markets that are of no interest to a potential bidder. In the screening process, it could be appropriate to assess how much of each candidate's operations relate to

- the target market for the bidding company
- other markets that could be of interest
- markets that are of no interest.

The possibility of selling off unwanted operations after a takeover should be considered. If a potential takeover candidate were to have significant operations in areas of no interest to the prospective bidder, and if these operations would be difficult to sell off except at a low price, the candidate probably would be eliminated during the screening process.

Ownership

Ownership of potential candidates could affect the screening process. It is important to establish who will have to be persuaded to accept a takeover bid. In a public company ownership could be widely held, or tightly controlled by a very small number of major shareholders. A company might have a history of successful defenses against hostile bids, indicating that an offer is likely to be rejected. Another company might have a history of joint ventures, suggesting that a joint venture proposal might have more success than a takeover bid.

In some small takeover bids, the targeted company's owners might be reluctant to sell. This is often the case, for example, among German Mittlestand companies that have been in family ownership for many years and where selling up can be seen as a sign of failure. The same considerations apply with Japanese target companies.

The financial position of the owners also can be a significant factor. When a company's owners have financial problems, they are more likely to be willing sellers.

Eliminating Candidates: First Screening

Potential takeover candidates can be eliminated according to their size, markets, product mix, spread of interests and ownership (availability). For several reasons, most candidates might be excluded at this stage, leaving the acquisitions team to focus on just one or two candidates. In the simplified example below, only company A out of six candidates identified as A to F, would survive the first screening process. The company could then be analyzed in further detail as a serious takeover prospect.

Illustrative screening process

Candidate	Size	Markets (Regional balance)	Product mix	Other activities outside targeted areas	Ownership (availability)
A					
B			X Only one product		
C		X Too focused			
D					X History of failed hostile bids
E	X Too small				X Single owner, unlikely to sell at acceptable price
F	X Too big			X Too much turnover in unrelated activities	

Performance Analysis of Target Company

From the information available, a performance analysis should be carried out on a takeover prospect. The purpose of this analysis should be to assess the value of the target company to the bidder, on the assumption that it remains a stand-alone business post-acquisition.

Company evaluations are difficult, and a variety of financial and non-financial performance criteria should be applied. These are suggested in the diagram.

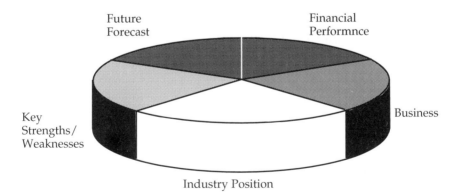

Future Forecast

Financial Performnce

Key Strengths/ Weaknesses

Business

Industry Position

Future Performance Forecast
Future growth prospects
Future margin improvements
Future cash flow generation
Potential risk areas

Key Strengths/Weaknesses
Products/brands
Technology
Assets
Management
Distribution

Industry Position
Cost structure compared with
  competitors
Competition
Positioning of supply chain

Financial Performance
Profit growth
Profit margins
Cash flow
Gearing
Yield
Other ratios

Business Performance
Market share
Product development
Geographical coverage
Innovation
Capital intensity
Assets (age/location etc.)
Employees

Synergy Analysis

There should be an analysis of the expected synergies from a takeover. The purpose of synergy analysis is to assess how much extra it might be worth to acquire the target company, in excess of its value as a stand-alone business, on the assumption that synergies could be achieved. It is worth including in this evaluation the financial benefits of preventing another potential purchaser from acquiring the target company.

The evaluation of synergies is a cost/benefit analysis. The benefits should come from lower costs such as common advertising or marketing costs, pooled R&D resources, or shared administration. The costs would be the additional capital investment and redundancy payments required to achieve the savings.

Strategic Benefits

The long-term or strategic benefits of an acquisition can be very difficult to evaluate. However, they could persuade a company to pay a higher price for an acquisition than the short-term value would justify.

Strategic benefits might include

- preventing acquisition of the target company by a competitor
- preventing acquisition of the bidding company by a larger competitor
- acquiring a strong brand name
- acquiring new technology skills.

If a value could be estimated for the strategic premium for an acquisition, the total value of the acquisition to the bidding company, that is the maximum price it should pay, would be as follows

Value of target as a stand-alone company	X
Net value of expected synergies	Y
Strategic premium	Z
Maximum offer price	X + Y + Z

Approaching a Target Company

Companies can approach a potential target company in one of three ways:

- a direct approach to the company's management
- an approach through advisers, such as an investment bank or firm of accountants
- an approach to a major shareholder of the target company, whose support would be sufficient for a bid to succeed. When the target of a bid is a subsidiary company in a group, the approach will be made to the parent company rather than to the subsidiary.

Negotiation Process

In a negotiated acquisition, the typical process for the bidding company, supported perhaps by advisers, is

- make an approach to the company's management
- set up a negotiating team
- sign a confidentiality letter. This is an undertaking by the bidding company not to make use of any information given to it by the target company, except for the purpose of formulating the bid
- receive a memorandum from the target company's management. This will contain confidential information about the target company, for example its sales history, profit margins, and sales and profit forecasts
- make an indicative bid. This is the price and purchase consideration that the bidder will offer, subject to satisfactory due diligence checks
- identify areas for investigation in the due diligence process
- carry out due diligence
- make a firm offer or a bid. A firm offer or pre-emptive bid is not a final bid, but is made on the understanding that the target company will not accept any offer from another bidder without first renegotiating the original offer.

Letter of Intent

In some purchase discussions, the buyer or the seller might ask for a formal acknowledgment of the seller's or buyer's intention to go through with the deal, even though a final agreement has not been reached. The seller might ask the buyer for a letter of intent, stating an intention to proceed with the purchase subject to certain events happening or conditions being fulfilled.

For example, Alcoa's 1998 acquisition of Spanish aluminum producer Inespal was agreed a year before it was completed. A letter of intent was signed in February 1997, and the details of the $410 million transaction were negotiated over the course of the next year.

In some negotiations, the seller might wish to defer the sale, but agree to give a bidder first refusal if it is eventually decided to sell.

Due Diligence

The purpose of a due diligence exercise is to confirm or revise the assumptions on which the takeover offer has been based. Normally due diligence is carried out when the target is a private (non-listed) company or the subsidiary company of a larger group. When the target is a listed company due diligence is often not possible and so the buyer will have to bid blind.

The major items to be checked will vary from one deal to another, but usually will include most of the following

- profit forecasts and cash forecasts
- the assumptions on which figures in the forecast are based
- prospects for synergy, economies from pooling resources after the takeover
- the actual existence of major customer sales contracts
- the existence and the condition of assets, their value and their legal ownership
- the target company's liabilities and potential liabilities
- confirmation that the target company is a going concern, and is operating normally
- confirmation that management and information systems are in place and continue to function properly
- investigation of any recent changes in the target company's financial structure or cash holdings.
- investigation into the current state of the target company's research and development operations
- environmental audit.

Due diligence must be carried out within a certain time period to avoid unacceptable delay in the takeover negotiations. The team set up to carry out due diligence must be large enough to do the work within the time available, and external advisers such as accountants, lawyers and environmental auditors generally would be employed. The due diligence team must insist on checking important matters, and should not use time pressure as an excuse for not doing so.

At the end of due diligence, the valuation of the target company and the offer price for the takeover should be reviewed. Due diligence could reveal that in some areas, the target company's position is worse than anticipated. The offer would then have to be reconsidered, with perhaps a revised offer or revised conditions.

The Offer Process

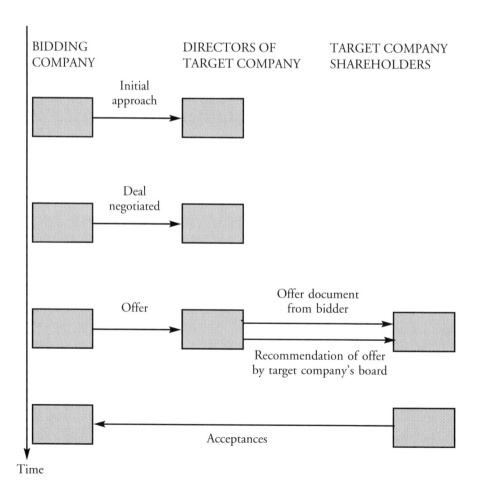

Offer Document

An offer document is a formal offer to acquire a company's shares. It is sent to the target company's shareholders, asking for their acceptance – an agreement to sell their shares. The document will include the offer terms. The bidder's post-acquisition plans for the company and the financial benefits of the acquisition also should be explained. In addition, the document should explain the commercial (strategic) justification for the acquisition, and the purchaser's intentions about continued employment for the target company's employees.

When the buyer is a quoted company, its advisers can suggest what price it can offer, without risking a sharp fall in the buyer's share price. The suggested price will reflect the buyer's estimate of profits from the acquired company and reorganization costs. This is one of the areas in which advisers can contribute significantly to the takeover process.

Areas of Difficulty

In any takeover negotiation, problem areas will arise. Most common, perhaps, is the difference in accounting policies between the bidding company and the target company.

Accounting Policies and Taxation

The bidder and the target might agree, for example, that the purchase price should be a multiple of annual profits, for example 10 times the most recent annual profits after tax. Different accounting policies could cause disagreement about the correct annual profit figure. Significant differences could be

- the rate of depreciation charges on fixed assets
- provisions for doubtful debts
- the accounting treatment of goodwill
- directors' salaries and other remuneration
- stock valuation policy.

Taxation is be a difficult area, especially in cross-border acquisitions.

Negotiations should take place to find agreement on how the profits of the target company should be measured for the purpose of the takeover valuation.

Special requirements or local factors also can create problems, for which solutions might have to be found. These will vary from one takeover bid to another. In a takeover of a small private company for example, the seller might insist that a company airplane or helicopter should be part of the sale, even though the bidder has no interest in the asset.

Warranties and Indemnities

When the target of a takeover bid is a private company, the bidder might require certain warranties and indemnities from the seller. The nature of these warranties and the consequences of any breach of warranty, must be agreed.

- A warranty is a form of guarantee in which an undertaking is given by the vendor to the purchaser. In the event that a breach of warranty occurs, and the promise has been broken, the purchaser has to demonstrate that a breach has occurred that qualifies the purchaser for damages/compensation. For example, the directors of a private company might warrant that any financial information that has been given to the vendor gives a true and fair view of their company's financial position at the time.
- An indemnity reinforces a warranty, and removes the onus on the purchaser to prove that a breach has occurred.

For example, the potential liabilities of the target company must be identified and assessed, if these are to be taken over. The bidding company might ask for a warranty from the seller that a potential liability will not exceed a certain amount, or for an indemnity from tax charges over a specified amount.

Other Major Issues

The major issues that could have to be clarified before agreement is reached vary from one deal to another. Typically in a negotiated takeover they will include an agreement about whether the offer price will be subject to adjustment, depending on specific outcomes. For example, the bidding company might agree to pay a specified sum for properties owned by the target company, subject to an independent valuation. The offer price might be based on a multiple of estimated profits, and subject to adjustment if actual profits for the period prove higher or lower than estimated.

Continuing Role of the Target Company's Management

A further major issue will be the role of the target company's management after the acquisition, and its pay and terms and conditions. If managers are worried about being made redundant, they could resist the takeover, or insist on adequate personal compensation. If the management is to remain in place after the takeover, it is essential to agree how much authority it will have, and how much will be assumed by the senior management of the bidding company.

Reorganization Costs

The bidding company might need to estimate the costs of planned reorganization and rationalization that would be required after the takeover has been completed. If redundancies are to be involved, the target company should be asked to provide details of how much these might cost (employment contract terms, etc.).

Potential Liabilities

The potential liabilities that a bidding company might have to take over post-acquisition vary widely. Some could be very costly. For example

- environmental costs, where the target company's operations are likely to require cleaning up or improving to meet environmental regulations, or political pressures for environmental improvements
- litigation
- a potential liability for payment of taxes for previous years
- medical insurance costs for retired employees

- employment contracts for staff in the target company
- liabilities under pension scheme arrangements
- potential inability of computer systems to integrate or to cope with new demands.

A pension scheme could entitle employees to a pension equal to a percentage of their final salary on retirement. An actuarial valuation should be undertaken to confirm that the target company's pension scheme has not been underfunded and will not require a top up at a later stage.

Reaching Agreement

The negotiating team in a takeover bid must have the authority to conclude an agreement. If matters continually have to be referred to a higher authority, confidence in the takeover discussions will evaporate.

The bidder must have the finance in place to support the bid. It would be irresponsible and damaging to agree an offer and subsequently find that finance is not available.

Misunderstandings should be avoided as much as possible. Each side should understand the other's objectives in the negotiations so that a deal can be struck that successfully achieves both parties' objectives. Major issues should be identified and clarified. Where appropriate, advisers should be appointed to help with identifying major issues and possible solutions. In cross-border acquisitions the bidder should appoint advisers with local knowledge of the country in which the target company operates.

Many takeover talks break down. A potential bidder must have patience, and should not try to secure a deal at all costs. Success is not guaranteed. If negotiations break down in the short term, the target company's management could ask to reopen talks, or be willing to consider a renewed offer at a later date.

Public Relations

In major takeovers, it is important to handle public relations carefully.
More specifically, it is often handled by the investor relations
department. Both sides in a negotiated takeover should agree their press
announcements. The benefits of the deal to both sides should be
explained in full.

Because major takeovers will attract stock market interest and press
comment, analysts and financial journalists should be given an
opportunity to attend question and answer sessions, to clarify the logic
and the attraction of the deal.

Valuations

A valuation of a target company or business is needed to decide the maximum price that a purchaser should be willing to pay for control. The seller responds to the offer that a bidder makes, based on the bidder's valuation. However, a seller also could make his own valuation of a shareholding or business unit, as the minimum cash price that would be acceptable or as the target price to achieve.

In a negotiated takeover, a buyer could start the bidding low, and raise the price as negotiations continue. In a hostile takeover, the bidder must try to decide a price from the outset that will persuade shareholders in the target company to sell. A hostile bid can be revised, but there is little opportunity to fine tune the price through negotiations.

There is neither any one correct method of valuation, nor a correct price. Different parties generally will have different views on value, reflecting different considerations. Price, not surprisingly, can be a stumbling block to successful negotiations. The seller often wants more than the buyer is willing to pay.

Bid Premium

When a purchaser takes over a listed company, the purchase price is almost invariably significantly higher than the current market capitalization of the target company. This premium is a prerequisite for persuading the shareholders to sell their shares to the bidder, rather than in the market.

From the bidder's point of view, it needs to be justified by the benefits of obtaining operational control. For example, being able to introduce benefits through synergies such as lower costs or higher revenues, will create extra value. The acquired company can be reorganized and its management systems improved. The challenge for the buyer is to ensure that the premium paid is not too high, and that the hoped-for synergy is in fact achieved.

Valuation Techniques

A number of valuation techniques can be used. Each technique produces a different valuation. Taken together, several different techniques could indicate the price level that a bidder should be willing to pay.

The valuation techniques are

- when the target is a listed company, current market capitalization plus bid premium
- when the bidder is a listed company, the relative size of the target company to that of the bidder
- Price/earnings ratio, or multiples of income before interest and tax or free cash flow, using historical bid analysis or comparative valuations of similar quoted companies
- discounted cash flow (DCF)
- asset value
- break-up value.

Several valuation techniques should be used. A single technique can be used to provide two or more different valuations, by altering the assumptions on which the calculations are based. All the techniques in the above list can be used to obtain a valuation for a listed company. However, techniques based on current market capitalization cannot be used for unlisted companies.

A purchaser should consider four values when the takeover target is a listed company, namely

- its current market capitalization
- the minimum price that would have to be offered to persuade shareholders to sell their shares
- the value of the benefits the purchaser would expect to obtain from a takeover, from extra profits or asset sales, etc. This sets a maximum price a purchaser ought to pay
- a target price that will be conceded through negotiation, probably representing a compromise between the highest price the buyer will pay and the lowest the sellers might accept.

Current Market Capitalization

When the target of a takeover bid is a listed company, the offer price must be higher than the current market price to have any chance of success. A bidder should expect to pay above the current market price to reflect a premium for gaining control of the target company.

Current market capitalization can be an unreliable guide when the share price of the target company is volatile, or the company is the subject of bid speculation.

Example
In April 1998 Citicorp and Travelers Group announced plans for a $166 billion merger to create the world's largest financial services company, to be known as Citigroup.

In the wake of the announcement shares in financial services companies rose sharply, amid speculation that other companies were potential takeover candidates. San Francisco-based Charles Schwab, for example, gained 6.9% on the announcement of the merger.

Historical Bid Analysis

It is sometimes possible to judge the likely size of the premium over current market value that a bidder can expect to pay for control, from an analysis of past successful bids in the industry. The percentage premium to current market value will be higher in some industries and parts of the world than in others.

Comparative Valuations

A valuation technique commonly used by M&A specialists in investment banks is to compare companies in the same industry using a variety of ratios. A judgment then can be made whether a particular company seems overvalued or undervalued compared to others. Undervalued companies could be recommended to clients as potential takeover targets, with some suggestion as to the offer price.

The comparative ratios in this type of analysis are concerned mainly with

- current market value, in relation to annual turnover, cash flow, profits and book value of assets
- operating margins, e.g. operating profit and net profit percentages
- the average annual growth rate in turnover, cash flows and profits over a period of about five years.

High-margin companies with a faster rate of growth and strong cash flows should have a higher rating than low-margin, low-growth businesses. Value comparisons therefore should take into consideration factors such as growth rates, the size of margins, quality of earnings and the strength of cash flows.

An example of comparative ratios that could be used in such circumstances is shown overleaf.

Company Comparisons

	Company A $ million	Company B $ million	Company C $ million	Company D $ million
Annual sales revenue	1,720.6	569.5	1,124.4	1,203.3
Operating cash flow	289.3	105.9	173.5	194.9
Operating income	258.1	91.2	146.2	150.4
Net income	103.3	34.7	48.0	29.7
Market values				
Equity capital	890.2	275.9	463.4	502.0
Preferred stock	50.0	0.0	0.0	0.0
Debt securities	200.0	0.0	0.0	50.0
Loans	66.0	74.5	240.0	147.7
	1,206.2	350.4	703.4	699.7
Cash and marketable securities	(27.8)	(8.6)	(9.3)	(12.1)
Total (current) value	1,178.4	341.8	694.1	687.6
Ratios				
Total value/annual sales	0.68	0.60	0.62	0.57
Total value/cash flow	4.1	3.2	4.0	3.5
Total value/operating income	4.6	3.7	4.7	4.6
Operating cash flow/ sales (%)	16.8	18.6	15.4	16.2
Operating income/sales, i.e. gross margin (%)	15.0	16.0	13.0	12.5
Net income/sales (%)	6.0	6.1	4.3	2.5
Book value per share	$0.40	$0.33	$0.43	$0.06
Market/book ratio	2.5	1.5	2.3	1.8
Five-year growth rates (% per annum)				
Sales revenue	8.2	10.5	6.1	8.4
Operating cash flow	7.6	6.7	8.3	7.3
Operating income	8.0	7.1	8.1	7.9
Net income	10.4	5.0	12.7	9.2

Definitions (for Ratio Analysis and Comparative Valuations)

The definition of items such as total market value and operating cash flow will differ between analysts.

The following definitions are suggested as a general guide.

- *Total enterprise value*

Current market value of shares based on mid-market price	A
Current market value of debt securities and preference shares	B
Face value of long-term loans	C
	A + B + C
Minus estimate of cash and marketable securities held	D
Total current market value	A + B + C - D

  The total enterprise value of a company, including loans and preferred stock, is needed to make proper comparisons of operating profits and cash flows. The current value of cash and marketable securities should be subtracted, because these do not contribute to the operating profit of the company and do not form part of its underlying value.

- *Operating cash flow*

Income before interest and taxation	A
Depreciation charges (a non-cash expense)	B
Operating cash flow	A + B

  In most countries, a more accurate measure of the operating cash flow of a company can be obtained from the cash flow statement in its published report and accounts.

- *Operating income and net income*
  Operating income is the income from operating activities, before deducting interest charges and tax. Net income is the income after taxation.

- *Book value per share*
  Book value is the value of the net assets of a company, as reported in its balance sheet. Book value represents, at an accounting valuation, the portion of the company owned by its equity shareholders. A book value per share is calculated by dividing the total book net asset value by the number of shares in issue.

Using Ratio Comparisons

Ratio comparisons can be used to identify both potentially undervalued companies, as well as those worth closer attention.

A useful but crude measure of comparative value is the market/book ratio. This is the ratio of the current market value of the company's equity shares to their book value. A comparatively low ratio might suggest an undervalued company. The ratio is very crude, however, because book values can be notoriously unreliable indicators of value.

In the following example, Company B could be worth close study by M&A advisers. Its market/book ratio is comparatively low. In addition

- the total value of the company is low in relation to its cash flows and operating profit
- its operating cash flow/sales ratio and operating profit/sales margin are both high
- it has achieved strong growth in annual sales, but slower growth in profits.

Once a company has been identified as undervalued, a potential bidder could assess what it might be worth if its performance could be improved to match those of its competitors.

Earnings Multiple or IBIT Multiple

A useful and simple valuation technique is to apply a multiple to either annual earnings (in broad terms, income after tax) or to annual income before interest and tax (IBIT). It is common practice to judge the value of a company on the basis of

- applying a value ratio to the most recent published annual earnings, excluding exceptional items (a historic P/E ratio or IBIT multiple), or
- applying a value ratio to expected earnings in the current year (a prospective P/E ratio or IBIT multiple).

This valuation technique is particularly useful for the purchase of private companies that do not have a measurable market value. A valuation can be negotiated by applying an agreed multiple to the company's most recent annual profits, or forecast profits for the current year. The multiple could be agreed by reference to

- the P/E ratios or IBIT multiples of public companies operating in the same industry
- exit P/E ratios on recent sales of similar companies, or
- the current P/E ratio or IBIT multiple of the bidding company.

A higher multiple can be appropriate for companies that are expecting high future growth and companies starting to recover from a business downturn.

The annual profits to which the multiple is applied will be subject to negotiation. Adjustments often are made for depreciation charges (applying the depreciation rates of the bidding company) and directors' salaries and other emoluments. Owner-directors of private companies could pay themselves high salaries, and for the purpose of agreeing a fair valuation, it is appropriate to substitute actual salaries with commercial, post-acquisition, salaries. Other adjustments may relate to exceptional or one-off profits or charges, and amortization of goodwill.

If the target company has an unusually high or low tax rate, a figure for earnings will be derived by applying an assumed normal rate of tax to pre-tax earnings.

Example
Alpha is negotiating with the three owner-directors of Beta for the purchase of their company. Beta's income is as follows:

	Previous year (actual)	Current year (estimate)
Income before tax	$700,000	$850,000
Income after tax (earnings)	$500,000	$600,000

Income is shown after deducting directors' emoluments of $300,000. Alpha's treasurer has estimated that using Alpha's own depreciation policies, the annual depreciation charge would be $50,000 higher.

Alpha's shares are priced in the stock market on a price/earnings ratio of 15. Its ratio of total enterprise value to income before interest and tax (IBIT multiple) is 11.5. The average P/E ratio for Alpha's industrial sector is 14.

Analysis
The valuation of Beta must be negotiated, and there is no one correct method. It could be that an agreement is reached to value Beta by applying a P/E ratio of 12, lower than Alpha's in recognition of Alpha's listed company status, to Beta's estimated current year pre-tax income, minus an estimated amount for taxation.

Also it might be agreed that a reasonable salary for the three directors should be $140,000, and that the profit figure should be adjusted

	$000
Income before tax (estimated)	850
Add directors' salaries (actual)	+300
	1,150
Deduct commercial salaries for directors	-140
	1,010
Depreciation policy adjustment	-50
Revised income before tax	960
Taxation (estimate 31%)	-298
Adjusted earnings	662

The valuation of Beta now will be

Annual earnings	x	P/E ratio
$662,000	x	12
= $7.94 million		

Earn-Outs (Valuation Based on Post-Acquisition Profits)

When private companies are taken over, and the agreed valuation is based on profits, the purchaser often will protect itself against disappointing profits post-acquisition by the purchased company. It is natural to suspect that the seller has massaged the company's profits in previous years with a view to sale, and has hidden key factors that will affect profit in the future, such as the need for substantial spending on modernization.

In an earn-out agreement, the purchase price consists of a minimum amount, payable immediately, plus one or more further payments at a future date, depending on the company's profitability in the period following the acquisition.

For example, a purchase price could be $20 million plus a further payment after three years that could be 12 times the amount by which profits before tax in year two exceed a stated figure.

When the former owners of the purchased company remain as directors post-acquisition, an earn-out agreement could motivate them to achieve substantial profit growth in the years following the takeover and up to the earn-out payment date.

Put and Call Options

Another valuation technique that links part of the purchase price for a private company to post-acquisition profits involves put and call options.

An arrangement could be made whereby the sellers of the company retain some shares. The buyer will acquire a controlling interest in the company. The sellers will become minority shareholders, and will probably remain as directors of the purchased company. The purchase agreement would include the issue of call options to the purchaser and put options to the seller.

- The call options would give the purchaser the right, but not the obligation, to buy the minority's shares for cash, on or after a specified date.
- The put options would give the minority shareholders the right,

but not the obligation, to sell their shares for cash to the majority shareholder, on or after a specified date.

The price formula for buying the shares if the call options were exercised, or for selling if the put options were exercised, should be written into the original acquisition agreement. The price formula usually will be based on the post-acquisition income of the acquired company, the post-acquisition income of the group as a whole, or the purchasing company's P/E ratio at the time the options are exercised.

Example

A joint venture is agreed between Lima Inc and Oscar, to import printing machinery into the US. A new joint venture company, Papa Inc, is set up with Lima owning 50.1% and Oscar 49.9%.

Lima and Oscar have put and call options over Oscar's share of the business, exercisable after four years and with a ceiling price on the value of any payment. Oscar therefore could require Lima to buy the shares, or Lima could require Oscar to sell the shares, at a price based on an agreed formula, subject to the price cap.

Weakness of P/E Ratio Valuation Technique

While P/E ratio valuation technique has the advantages of speed and simplicity, it also has several weaknesses

- accounting policies vary between companies, and their reported earnings are therefore calculated on different bases
- the P/E ratios of individual companies reflect the market's expectations of future earnings growth. This differs between companies, making comparisons difficult
- different companies have different capital structures. Financial leverage affects the perceived risk, and therefore the market value and the P/E ratio of a company. This difficulty can be addressed to an extent by valuing using earnings before interest multiples rather than net income.

Free Cash Flow Multiple

Companies with strong positive operational cash flows could be valued on a multiple of their free cash flow. Free cash flow is the company's net operating cash flows minus any non-operational cash payments that it has to make, for example interest costs and payments of corporate taxes.

Discounted Cash Flow Valuation

The most scientific method of valuation in common use is the discounted cash flow (DCF) method. DCF is a financial technique to evaluate the financial costs and benefits of long-term investments, or to estimate the value of an investment, such as a long-term acquisition. It can be used to make a company valuation, based on the anticipated free cash flows of the company over a number of years. It is particularly suitable for the valuation of target companies that own product rights with a limited life span, such as patents on medical products, or in any instance where reliable cash flow forecasts are available.

Making a DCF Valuation

To make a DCF valuation

- construct a profile of the anticipated free cash flows of the target company over the chosen investment period/payback period. Free cash flow can be estimated as profits after taxation, plus depreciation charges
- estimate, in cash flow terms, the expected benefits from synergy such as cost savings, etc.
- allow for any anticipated rationalization costs, or new investments that would be required in fixed assets (new equipment) or working capital (stocks and debtors)
- allow for any anticipated benefits from the resale of an asset or part of the acquired company
- decide what the average annual return on the investment should be

over the payback period, expressed as an annual rate of interest per annum. This is the target investment yield, and may be based on the purchaser's cost of capital

● make the present value calculation.

Estimating Cash Flows

Estimating the cash flows from an investment inevitably is subject to some uncertainty, especially because the cash flows need to be projected several years into the future. A reasonable estimate of the extra cash flows from acquiring a company would be

The pre-tax profits of the subsidiary	A
Annual depreciation	+ B
Additions to profits from synergy benefits	+ C
Less taxation on profits	- (D)
	A + B + C - D

In addition cash flows also should provide for any cost of post-acquisition rationalization measures. These should include the cost of redundancies and the revenue from disposal of unwanted assets or business units.

A DCF valuation, as its name implies, is based on estimated cash flows, not profits. Cash flows are, generally speaking, income plus annual depreciation costs. Depreciation is not a cash flow. It is an annual charge for the use and wearing out of fixed assets that have already been bought. In DCF, the purchase cost of an investment is included in the cash flows, and so to include depreciation as an annual expense would be double counting.

Estimated cash flows should be divided into time periods. It is common, but not essential, to estimate annual cash flows. In DCF, an annual cash flow is assumed to occur at the end of the year to which it relates. Cash flows for Year 1, for example, are assumed to occur at the end of Year 1, whereas in reality they occur throughout the year.

Cash flows that occur early in the year can be assumed to occur at the end of the previous year. For example, cash flows at or near the start of an investment, including the cost of the investment itself, are assumed to occur at the end of Year 0, i.e. at the start of Year 1.

Investment Payback Period

Some companies will decide on a maximum payback period for an investment. This could be ten years or five years. The valuation of an investment should then be based on cash flows only up to the end of the payback period. This assumes that the company will not pay for cash flows generated after the end of their payback period.

Alternatively, when valuing a target company, an estimate can be made of average annual cash flows beyond the forecast period into perpetuity and this figure then can be added to the DCF calculation as a one-off terminal value. This terminal value can add up to a substantial part of the total value, so the assumptions behind these estimated cash flows should be very carefully considered.

Discount Rate

The discount rate also must be decided. From a buyer's point of view, this is the average annual percentage rate of return that he requires from the investment.

For bidder companies using DCF valuation techniques, the board of directors usually fixes the required investment return on major projects. There are different methods of measuring a required rate of return. One method is to measure the company's weighted cost of funds. This is the weighted average return required by the company's shareholders and lenders. Provided all investments achieve this return, the company can continue to pay the yields that its providers of finance demand.

Another method of measuring the required rate of return is to adjust the cost of funds by a project risk factor. High-risk projects would be required to yield a higher return than low-risk projects. Also it might be adjusted if the target company were funded differently to the bidder, i.e. if its particular cost of capital is greater or less than the bidder's. Sometimes a higher discount rate may be used in calculating a terminal value to reflect higher risk in a more distant period.

From the seller's point of view, the discount rate usually will reflect his own cost of capital.

DCF Mathematics

The mathematics of DCF are straightforward. Capital investment decisions involve spending money to obtain returns years into the future. To evaluate an investment, the time value of money must be taken into account. A dollar that will be earned in the future is worth less than a dollar earned today because money can be reinvested to earn more over time. For example, at an investment rate of 10% per annum, $110 in one year's time is the equivalent of $100 now.

Cash flows earned in the future can be converted to a present value equivalent by means of discounting. The formula for converting a cash flow in a future year to its present value equivalent is

$$PV_o = FV_n \times \frac{1}{(1+r)^n}$$

Where

- PV_o is the present investment value of a future cash flow, i.e. its value in Year 0
- FV_n is the future cash flow in Year n
- n is the year of the cash flow
- r is the investment rate, discount rate or cost of capital, expressed as a proportion (10% is 0.10, 7% is 0.07, etc.)

For example, the present value of $110 at the end of Year 1, at an investment rate of 10% per annum, is

$$PV = \$110 \times \frac{1}{(1.10)^1} = \$100$$

The present value of all the expected future cash flows from an investment project is the amount of money that would have to be invested now to earn those future cash flows, if the investment rate of return is the cost of capital.

By discounting the expected net cash flows from an acquisition, at the required investment rate of return, a valuation can be obtained for the target company. The valuation is simply the present value of the future cash flows, up to the end of the purchasing company's maximum payback period.

If a terminal value is included in the valuation, this is shown in the final year of the cash flow, and calculated as

$$TV = \frac{FV_n + g}{r - g}$$

Where g = expected growth into perpetuity.

Example

Echo wishes to take over Foxtrot. It is expected that the extra cash flows from the acquisition will be as follows, after allowing for synergy benefits and corporate taxation

Year	Cash flows
	$m
1	10
2	15
3	20
4	25
5	25

There will be reorganization costs after the takeover, estimated at $6 million soon after the acquisition and $12 million about one year later. Also there will be a requirement early in Year 1 to invest a further $5 million in new equipment for Foxtrot. Echo plc expects all its acquisitions to earn an investment return of 12% per annum. Cash flows are expected to be at around $20 million per annum after Year 5, and a higher discount rate of 14% is to be applied to these.

Analysis

The estimated cash flows from the acquisition should be discounted to a present value, at an investment rate of 12% per annum, to assess their investment value to the buyer.

Year	Operational cash flows	Reorganization costs	New investment	Net cash flow	Discount factor at 12%	Present value
	$m	$m	$m	$m		$m
0	–	(6)	(5)	(11)	1.0	(11.00)
1	10	(12)		(2)	$\dfrac{1}{(1.12)^1}$	(1.79)
2	15	–		15	$\dfrac{1}{(1.12)^2}$	11.96
3	20	–		20	$\dfrac{1}{(1.12)^3}$	14.24
4	25	–		25	$\dfrac{1}{(1.12)^4}$	15.89
5	25	–		25	$\dfrac{1}{(1.12)^5}$	14.19
5 (TV)	143 (i.e. 20÷0.14)	–		143	$\dfrac{1}{(1.12)^5}$	81.06
					Net present value	124.55

The present value of the cash flows, $124.55 million, is the valuation of the Foxtrot acquisition. This value indicates the maximum price that Echo should perhaps be willing to offer.

Uncertainty in Cash Flows

Despite the investment mathematics, DCF valuations are a matter of judgment, supported however by assumptions on which cash flows and present values are calculated. If the cash flows are unreliable, a DCF valuation is meaningless. The assumptions on which estimated cash flows have been based should be checked carefully, and clearly specified.

It is sensible to carry out several DCF valuations, each using a different set of assumptions. For example, three separate valuations could be produced using pessimistic, optimistic and most likely assumptions about what will occur after the acquisition is made. These will provide a range of valuations that should help the negotiating team to assess

- the initial price they might bid based on pessimistic assumptions
- a price that they can negotiate comfortably based on the most likely assumptions
- the maximum price they ought to bid based on what are considered to be optimistic assumptions.

Break-Up Value

Some takeovers are proposed with the intention of breaking up the acquired company and selling off its businesses or assets separately to different buyers. Companies with a large asset base and poor profitability can be prime candidates for such a bid. Their market capitalization is likely to be low, and the market/book value ratio also will be low.

Profits can be made from

- asset stripping, or
- breaking up the business.

Asset stripping means buying the company at a small premium to its current market price and stripping out, or selling off, its most valuable assets at a profit – selling off property that was undervalued in the target company's balance sheet. The remaining shell of the company might then be liquidated.

5

Structuring a
Takeover Deal

When contemplating a bid, a company has to decide not just the valuation of a target company and the price to offer, but also how to structure and finance the payment.

There are three main financial aspects to structuring an acquisition

- deciding whether to bid for the target company's assets only, or for the target company's stocks
- the purchase consideration, that is the form the purchase price should take
- the financing package to provide the purchase consideration.

When involved in a merger, a major issue is to agree a corporate structure and stockholding structure for the merged enterprise.

Assets or Stocks?

In a negotiated takeover, the buyer and the vendors must reach an agreement about whether the buyer will acquire a company's stocks, or just specified assets and liabilities.

When a target company's stocks are purchased, the acquirer obtains all the company's rights, liabilities and contingent liabilities. When the target company is the subsidiary of a parent company, there may be outstanding intercompany loans between the subsidiary and the parent or other group companies. A condition of the takeover could then be a requirement that these loans should be repaid.

If the target company has a large amount of cash or near-cash assets, there must be agreement on whether this money, and how much of it, can be taken out by the company's owners before the purchase takes place.

By negotiating to buy specified assets of a company, a purchaser can be selective about which assets and liabilities to acquire. The sale of assets or businesses is quite common in cases where a company wishes to sell off unwanted businesses. A buyer might agree to acquire the assets and some liabilities for example, agree to pay trade creditors, but decline to take on other assets or liabilities such as the lease on unwanted property.

Tax Implications

The preference for acquiring the company's stocks or just selected assets will be influenced by possible tax implications. When the purchaser buys the entire company

- the purchased company's tax reliefs also are acquired
- the purchaser also will take on the acquired company's tax liabilities. Indemnities should be sought from the vendor company about the maximum potential size of these liabilities
- any capital gain that is taxable, is attributed to the individual stockholders of the vendor company, and not to the vendor company itself.

When the purchaser buys selected assets of the target company, any tax liability on the capital gain is attributed to the target company, not the selling stockholders. The company's management therefore will need to consider whether these capital gains can be offset, to reduce or eliminate any tax liability.

Example
In 1997 a merger between German banks Bayerische Vereinsbank and Bayerische Hypo-Bank highlighted the advantages of efficient tax-structure. In structuring the transaction as an asset-swap, the banks

were able to avoid a substantial capital gains tax bill. To qualify, assets had to be of equal value, of equal type and of equal function, for example a swap of stocks in two financial companies.

As a general guide, an acquisition involving the purchase of the assets and trade of a target business is more likely to occur when

- the target business is part of a larger organization
- the deal is not a complex one.

The Purchase Consideration

The purchase price of an acquired company could be in the form of

- cash
- paper
- a mixture of cash and paper
- a choice between cash or paper, as preferred by individual stockholders in the target company.

Paper is usually in the form of newly issued stocks of the bidding company, but also could be debenture stock (loan stock), preferred stock, convertible stock, or stock warrants.

Cash offers could involve stocks being paid for out of the bidder's own funds. To finance large acquisitions the bidder often must borrow in the capital markets by issuing medium-term notes, bonds or even commercial paper. Alternatively, banks may be willing to provide loans to finance acquisitions.

When making a substantial bid, a quoted company's management often will require support from its bankers, stock market advisers or stockholders. To make a cash offer financed by a bank loan or capital market issue of bonds or stocks, etc., the cash will not be available unless the bank is willing to lend, or the company's stock market sponsors are willing to support a new issue. Stockholder approval may be required to issue new stocks as purchase consideration for a takeover.

Purchase Consideration

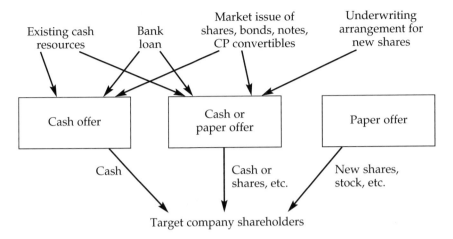

Cash Offers

When a company has sufficient cash to pay the purchase price in full, a takeover usually can be achieved quickly and at a low cost, fees for advisers, such as accountants and lawyers, should be low. In addition, confidentiality probably will be better maintained.

There can be regulatory restrictions, even for cash offers, depending on the country concerned.

Financing a Cash Offer

If a company wishes to finance a cash offer with bank loans, or if there are restrictive covenants on existing loans that prohibit acquisitions without the lending banks' approval, obtaining bank support for the takeover can be a lengthy process. Ultimately it will depend on the number of banks involved and the terms of the takeover.

A company seeking a large bank loan could try to reduce likely delays and inconvenience by arranging a bilateral loan with just one bank, leaving the bank to syndicate the loan by arranging sub-participation in the loan by other banks.

Bankers should be aware of national laws that can affect a lending arrangement to support a takeover bid. In most countries, it is an offence for a company to provide financial assistance for the purchase of its own stocks. Suppose, for example, that Alpha wants to acquire Beta and negotiates a bank loan to finance the purchase. As security for the loan, Alpha cannot offer the bank any of the assets of Beta, because Beta would be giving financial assistance for the purchase of its stocks. If Beta were allowed to offer its assets as security, the position of Beta's creditors would be put at risk.

Takeovers that involve borrowing in the bond markets to pay for an acquisition have been comparatively rare in the past few years. One such example was the 1998 purchase by US aluminum producer Alcoa of Spain's largest aluminum company, Inespal, for $410 million. Alcoa agreed to invest 65 billion pesetas in the business over ten years. The deal was part financed by the sale of $300 million of 30-year senior unsecured debt with the balance drawn from Alcoa's own cash reserves.

Issuing new stocks to raise the required cash also could finance a cash offer. Stockholder or investor approval for the bid would be required, and the securities house sponsoring the stock issue will expect the company to present a convincing economic argument for the takeover.

When a company is small, and owned by a restricted number of stockholders, financing acquisitions by placing stocks with external investors can have the significant advantage of widening stock ownership in the company, thereby helping to make its stocks more liquid in secondary stock market trading.

Occasionally, a subsidiary of a larger parent company makes an acquisition in which the cash purchase consideration is financed by an issue of new stocks in the subsidiary. This situation can arise when the subsidiary is a public company with a stock market listing. If the parent company also wishes to reduce its percentage stake in the subsidiary, this method of financing an acquisition would be preferred because all new stocks could be offered to other investors.

Example

Alpha, a company controlled by Papa Inc., announces an agreement to buy a rival company, Bravo Ltd. The agreed price is $300 million.

To finance the deal, Alpha issues 10 million new stocks to raise about $300 million. Papa will not buy any of the stocks, and its stake in Alpha therefore falls.

Cash Underwriting (Vendor Placement)

In situations where the owners of the target company (the vendors) want cash, and the purchasing company cannot raise the money from existing cash resources or by borrowing, an arrangement could be agreed whereby

- the vendors accept stocks in the purchasing company, and
- the stocks are immediately placed with buyers who are usually institutional investors, who have agreed to take up the stocks.

This arrangement is known as a vendor placement or vendor placing.

Paper Offers

In a paper offer, the target company's stockholders are asked to surrender ownership of their stocks for new stocks or loan stock issued by the bidding company. For instance, target company stockholders could be offered x new stocks in the bidding company in exchange for every stock they hold.

Stock-For-Stock Swaps

In a stock-for-stock swap, a merger or takeover can take place without any cash changing hands. As a result, the stockholders of the acquired company will be stockholders in the post-acquisition company. A stock-for-stock offer will be acceptable to the target company's stockholders only if

- they want to hold an equity stake in the purchasing company, i.e. if the bidder represents an attractive investment
- they expect to resell the stocks on the stock market after the acquisition, and obtain a cash consideration
- they are keen to sell their existing stocks and a paper offer is all that they receive.

Example

In December 1996 Boeing and McDonnell Douglas announced their plan to merge to become the world's leading aerospace and defense company, under the Boeing name. Boeing offered McDonnell Douglas a stock swap of 0.65 Boeing stocks for each McDonnell Douglas stock held, valuing the company at $13.3 billion.

Price Risk

In a stock-for-stock takeover, there is some price risk for the purchaser during the negotiating period when a valuation for the takeover is agreed. The risk is that the market price of the purchasing company's stocks will fall during the period. As a consequence, the company will have to offer more of its stocks in the offer.

Example

Negotiations take place between Echo and Foxtrot Inc. for the acquisition of Foxtrot by Echo. A valuation of $6 million is agreed during the discussions, with a stock-for-stock swap as the purchase consideration. Foxtrot has one million stocks in issue and each is valued at $6 in the takeover offer. Echo's stocks will be valued at their mid-market price as at the end of market trading on the day before the final purchase agreement is signed. This will be in about one week's time. The current market price of Echo's stocks is $3.

Analysis

If Echo's stock price remains unchanged at $3, the purchase consideration will be two million stocks ($6 million ÷ $3 per stock).

There is a risk, however, that Echo's stock price could fall before the deal is signed. If it fell, for example, to $2.75, Echo would need to issue more stocks to pay for the takeover, issuing 2,181,818 stocks ($6 million ÷ $2.75 per stock) instead of two million.

There is also a price risk between the time of agreeing the offer details and obtaining acceptance from the target company's stockholders. During this short but critical period when the offer is put to stockholders, a fall in stock price will increase the risk of the offer being rejected because the value of the bid will go down.

Example
In November 1996 British Telecommunications plc and US long-distance carrier MCI communications announced a merger that would create the world's largest telecommunications group, to be named Concert. The purchase price for the 80% of MCI that BT did not already own was over $20 billion, comprising

- 5.4 Concert stocks plus
- $6 cash per MCI stock, valuing the stocks at around $36.

However in July 1997 MCI issued a profits warning that resulted in its stock price falling to $20, reducing MCI's market capitalization by about $6 billion. Although highly unusual, BT's institutional stockholders demanded a renegotiation of the terms of the merger and eventually revised terms were agreed as follows

- 3.75 Concert stocks plus
- $7.75 cash per MCI stock, valuing the stocks at around $35.

BT's bid for MCI was then trumped in October 1997 by a rival bidder, WorldCom, that offered $30 billion for MCI in an all-paper offer. WorldCom's offer was structured so as to protect investors from the effects of movements in WorldCom's stock price. Under this initial offer, MCI stockholders would have received

- at least 1.0375 WorldCom stocks, if WorldCom's average price in the 20 days before completion was above $40, or

- no more than 1.2206 stocks if WorldCom's stock price was below $34, and
- if the WorldCom stock price was between $34 and $40 the number of stocks issued was to vary to provide MCI holders with a fixed value of $41.50.

The purchasing company's stock price may be weak when a large takeover bid has been announced and also soon after completing the acquisition. This would be because of suspicion among investors that the purchaser had paid a large premium above true value to acquire the stocks, particularly if there were competing bids for the same company. Also, there could be a suspicion that the target company's former stockholders, who had accepted stocks in the purchasing company, would not hold them long, that there would be an overhang of stocks in the market. The threat of large selling orders in the stock market for the company's stocks could keep the price subdued for some time.

Other Paper Offers

The purchaser can offer preference stocks, loan stock or convertible securities (loans or preferred stocks) as consideration, or as part of the consideration, for a takeover. The stockholders of the purchased company are offered neither cash nor equity for their stocks, except in the case of convertible securities, when equity stocks will be offered at some future time. The dividend or interest payable, the term to maturity and terms of conversion will affect the attractiveness of the securities and will have to be agreed in the offer talks.

Loan stock can be offered in a variety of forms, for example as debenture stock or loan notes. Loan notes are interest-bearing debt, often unsecured and with no covenants. They constitute a promise by the purchasing company to pay an agreed amount at a future date, when the notes mature. In effect, financing a takeover with a stocks-for-loan notes swap means that the stockholders of the acquired company are financing the purchase of their company.

The acceptance of loan stock as all or part of the purchase consideration means that the seller believes the buyer is creditworthy and will pay the debt at maturity.

Convertible loan stock offers the vendor stockholders the choice between a deferred payment for their stocks, when the loan stock matures, and the carrot of converting their stock into equity stocks of the purchasing company at a future date, and at a fixed rate of conversion. If the stock price rises substantially during the time between the acquisition and the date for exercising conversion rights, the holders of the convertibles can benefit by exchanging their loan stock for stocks. At worst, they will not exercise their conversion rights, and will receive cash for their loan stock at maturity.

An alternative to offering convertible loan stock is to offer loan stock with stock warrants attached. The stock warrants would give the holders the right to subscribe for new stocks in the purchasing company at a future date, at a fixed price. Stock warrants have the same advantage as convertible loan stock, allowing their holders to benefit from an increase in the purchasing company's stock price in the period up to the warrant exercise date. A further significant attraction of stock warrants is that they can be detached and traded separately. Stock market listings for stock warrants can be obtained.

Mixed Offers

Mixed offers of part cash and part paper are made when the purchaser does not have enough cash to pay for the acquisition, and is unable, or does not wish to raise cash by borrowing or issuing new stocks. A mixed offer is therefore a purchase consideration package that the purchaser is able, or willing, to afford. In the takeover of a small company where the owner-directors will remain as managers after the acquisition, the buyers could ask the sellers to take some of the purchase consideration in stocks, and to hold the stocks for a minimum number of years. This would be a token sign of support and commitment to the new group.

There is a risk with cash-and-paper offers, as with all-paper offers, that the bidder's stock price could fall, reducing the value of the bid and making acceptance by the target company's stockholders less likely.

Paper or Cash Alternative

An offer can be made giving the target company's stockholders a choice between accepting cash or the purchasing company's stocks. A paper offer with a cash alternative can be attractive to vendors because of the choice it gives, improving the likelihood that the bid will be accepted.

Underwriting

When the purchase consideration includes a cash alternative, the purchaser will not know how many stocks will be accepted by the target company stockholders, and how many will prefer cash. The company might arrange for an issue of new stocks to be underwritten, up to a maximum number of stocks. To the extent that the target company stockholders opt for payment in cash, new stocks will be placed with the underwriters to raise the money.

Deciding on the Purchase Consideration

In a friendly negotiated bid, the management or stockholders of the target company will indicate how they wish to be paid: in cash, in paper, or a mix of cash and paper. Their preference usually will influence the bidder's offer. In a hostile bid, the bidder must offer a price and purchase consideration that it expects the target company's stockholders to accept, despite the opposition from the company's board of directors.

The choice of purchase consideration can be affected by a number of factors that will make the bidder inclined to offer cash or the vendor willing to accept paper. These include

- the bid premium
- the liquidity/marketability of the bidding company's stocks
- the requirement for speed and confidentiality

- individual tax considerations
- legal or regulatory issues
- market conditions
- competition from rival bidders for the company.

As a general guide, if the market is not receptive to a company's paper, it will be extremely difficult for the company to finance a takeover by issuing new paper.

Acquisition Premium
If the bidder is willing to pay a higher price than it would for a cash offer, that is if the bidder pays a higher premium for the acquisition, it can try to insist on a paper offer or a mixed cash and paper offer. The target company's stockholders could be willing to accept a paper offer to obtain a better price.

Liquidity/Marketability of the Bidder's Stocks
If the bidding company's stocks are liquid, meaning they can be traded easily in the stock market, the target company's stockholders will be more willing to accept a paper offer than if the bidding company's stocks were not liquid. Easily marketable stocks can be readily sold for cash, whereas stocks that are not liquid can be difficult to sell. A paper offer of liquid stocks would be almost as good as a cash offer but with some price risk, the risk that the stock price could fall before they are sold.

When the bidding company's stocks do not have a local stock market listing, and are therefore not liquid, the seller usually will want to be paid in cash. For example, acquisitions in the UK by subsidiaries of US or Japanese companies usually will be paid for in cash.

Speed and Confidentiality
If the bidding company wishes to complete an acquisition quickly and with as much confidentiality as possible, it could decide to make a cash offer, with the money coming from existing cash resources or bank borrowing facilities. A cash offer from existing resources avoids the need

to arrange new finance or to obtain stockholder approval for an issue of new stocks.

Tax

The rules for tax on capital gains could make a stock offer attractive to a target company's stockholders. If they sell their stocks for a higher price than they originally paid for them, there is a capital gain that is subject to tax. In the UK, the gain is taxable in the year of sale when the purchase consideration is cash. However, by accepting a stock offer, the vendors can roll over the capital gains tax liability that becomes payable only when and if the stocks are sold.

Convertible loan stock also may be attractive to vendors for tax reasons because it may be possible to convert the stock in stages, in order to use up annual tax exemptions and reduce the total tax payable.

Legal and Regulatory Issues

Legal and regulatory issues that vary between countries, can affect the make-up of the purchase consideration.

Market Conditions

If there is a strong economic argument supporting a takeover bid, the bidding company should be able to issue stocks or other paper to raise cash for the purchase consideration. Conditions in the markets could affect the price at which the equities or bonds would have to be issued. Doubts about general economic prospects, high interest rates or a shortage of cash among institutional investors could affect the cost of funds. If the cost of funds is fairly low, and investors are confident about business prospects, a bidder could be more willing to consider cash bids for takeovers, financed by a stock or bond issue.

Competition from Rival Bidders

When two or more companies are competing to acquire a target company, each could raise its offer price, to leapfrog over its rival's most recent price. There are two other ways of making one bid more attractive than the other

- offering cash rather than paper
- offering a higher price, but in the form of paper.

Example

After WorldCom made its all-paper $41.50 per stock bid for MCI, a further rival bidder appeared on the scene during October 1997. This was GTE that made a lower $40 per stock all-cash offer for MCI on the basis that cash would be more attractive to MCI stockholders than WorldCom paper.

Deciding on the Financing Package

The financing of an acquisition from existing cash, by issuing stocks, bonds or convertibles, or by bank borrowing, has significant implications for the bidding company's financial position after the takeover. The two most significant financial issues are the effect of the takeover on

- earnings per share, and
- leverage.

In addition, a company also should consider the effects on its earnings and leverage of any other fund raising that it has planned.

There can be financial reporting issues to consider also, and these are discussed in Chapter 9.

Earnings per Share

An acquisition will have an impact on the purchasing company's earnings per share. On the assumption that the annual income before interest and tax of the purchasing company and the acquired company are the same post-acquisition as pre-acquisition, there will be either

- earnings enhancement (earnings per share will increase), or
- earnings dilution (earnings per share will fall).

Some earnings enhancement or dilution will occur with both cash and paper offers. For a company wishing to finance a takeover with a stock issue for cash, investors will be more willing to support a takeover that is earnings-enhancing, and will need convincing that an earnings-dilutive takeover would be beneficial in the long term.

Earnings Enhancement

Earnings enhancement will occur in various situations such as

- when the purchase is financed from existing cash resources and the acquired company's profits exceed the interest receivable from investing the cash
- when the purchase is financed by issuing stocks, and the price paid for the target company's stocks is at a lower earnings multiple than the P/E ratio of the purchasing company
- when the purchase is financed by borrowing or issuing loan stock, and the profits from the acquired company exceed the interest cost of the finance.

Earnings enhancement also can occur when the takeover enhances profits through synergy such as cost savings, etc.

Example

Sierra, a public company, acquires Tango Inc., a private company. The purchase consideration was ten million stocks in Sierra. Tango's annual profits after earnings were $3 million.

Before the acquisition, Sierra Inc. had 200 million stocks in issue. Sierra's annual profits before tax were $40 million, so that earnings per stock were $0.20 ($40 million ÷ 200 million). The stock price of Sierra at the time of the acquisition was $3. The price/earnings ratio of Sierra's stocks was therefore 15 ($3 ÷ $0.20).

Analysis

The valuation of Tango at the time of the acquisition was $30 million (10 million Sierra stocks as purchase consideration, at $3 per stock). Tango's profits were $3 million. Tango therefore was valued at an earnings multiple of 10. This is the price/earnings ratio between the valuation of $30 million and the annual profits of $3 million.

Sierra's price/earnings ratio was 15, that is higher. This means that if the post-acquisition profits of Sierra are the same as the combined pre-acquisition profits of Sierra and Tango, i.e. there is no profit enhancement through synergy, there will be earnings enhancement for Sierra from the acquisition, as shown.

	Sierra pre-acquisition	Sierra post-acquisition
Annual profit	$40 million	$43 million
Number of shares	200 million	210 million
Earnings per share	$0.20	$0.205

There is an earnings enhancement of 2.5%, from $0.20 per share to $0.205 per share.

If Sierra's share price maintains its price/earnings multiple of 15, the share price will rise by 2.5% to $3.075 ($0.205 x 15).

Earnings Dilution

Earnings dilution occurs in the opposite situations to earnings enhancement, such as

- when the purchase is financed from existing cash resources, and the acquired company's income is less than the interest that could be earned by investing the cash
- when the purchase is financed by a stock issue, and the target company's shares are valued on a higher price/earnings ratio (earnings multiple) than the purchasing company's shares
- when the purchase is financed by issuing paper other than equity, and the acquired company's profits are less than the interest or dividend costs on the new paper

- when operational difficulties, post-acquisition, result in falling profits for either company.

Dilution and the Stock Price

When earnings dilution is expected from an acquisition, the company's stock price is likely to fall. An expected dilution in earnings of 5%, for example, could result in the stock price also falling by about 5% or even more in some cases.

If a company issues new stocks to finance an acquisition, the subscription price will be lower than the current market price. This is necessary to win investor support for a stock placement or rights issue. Issuing new stocks at a discount to the current market value can be earnings-dilutive.

Example

Leo Inc. had 25 million stocks in issue, priced at $4.30 each. Its market capitalization therefore was $107.5 million (25 million x $4.30). The most recent year's net income after tax was $10.75 million, valuing the company on a historic P/E ratio of 10.

Leo acquired 100% of the stock capital of Oscar for $7.8 million. The purchase consideration was paid entirely in cash that Leo raised by issuing two million new stocks at $3.90 each. Oscar's latest reported net profit after tax was $0.78 million, valuing the company on the same historic P/E ratio as Leo, i.e. 10.

Analysis

Because Leo and Oscar are both valued on the same P/E ratio of 10, there should be no earnings dilution for Leo from the acquisition. However, by issuing new stocks at a discount to their current market price, some earnings dilution can be expected. In addition, there may be a subsequent fall in Leo stock price.

	Leo pre-acquisition	Leo post-acquisition
Annual earnings	$10.75 million	$11.53 million (10.75 + 0.78)
Number of stocks	25 million	27 million
Earnings per stock	$0.43	$0.427

There will be a fall in earnings per stock of 0.7%, from $0.43 to $0.427.

Because two million stocks are being issued at $3.90, 9.3% below the current market price of $4.30, most probably there will be some fall in Leo's stock price after the issue. However, the actual post-acquisition price will depend on the market's perceptions of the company's prospects as a consequence of the takeover.

Earnings and Post-Acquisition Synergy

Earnings dilution can be expected whenever a purchasing company offers a high price to acquire a target company. Cost savings or other profit growth from post-acquisition synergy can offset this. Earnings dilution therefore can be reduced, or even prevented altogether, by post-acquisition rationalization. Quite often, a purchasing company will undertake a radical cost-cutting exercise after an acquisition in order to improve profitability.

Example

Romeo Inc. had 50 million stocks in issue, priced at $4 each. Its latest net profit was $0.50 per stock ($25 million in total). Romeo's P/E ratio was eight ($4 ÷ $0.50).

Victor Limited had net profits of $6 million. Romeo purchased Victor for $72 million, valuing the company on a P/E ratio of 12 ($72 million ÷ $6 million). The purchase consideration was 18 million Romeo stocks. Post-acquisition synergies are expected to reduce costs and increase annual earnings by $4 million.

Analysis

	Romeo pre-acquisition	Romeo post-acquisition no synergy	Romeo post-acquisition, with synergy
Annual earnings	$m	$m	$m
Pre-acquisition	25	25	25
From Victor	-	6	6
From synergy	-	-	4
Total earnings	25	31	35
Stocks	50 million	68 million	68 million
Earnings per stock	$0.50	$0.456	$0.515

Without the synergy, the acquisition would dilute Romeo's earnings, because Victor was bought on a higher P/E ratio. With the cost savings, however, Romeo's earnings per stock will rise. Romeo should benefit from earnings enhancement, with earnings per stock rising by 3%, from $0.50 to $0.515.

Acquisitions and Leverage

Leverage is the ratio of debt to equity, expressed as a percentage, in a company's finance structure. High leverage is associated with greater financial risk for two reasons

- a very highly leveraged company is a potential credit risk because it might be unable to repay its debts or interest on schedule
- annual earnings for stockholders generally are more volatile as leverage increases.

Additionally, a highly geared company may find its ability to raise further expansion finance to be restricted. Following an acquisition a company often will comment about the post-acquisition leverage level in order to reassure investors.

When a company has a low level of net assets (assets minus liabilities), and needs to raise new finance to pay for a cash acquisition, it will try to raise the money with a stock issue rather than by borrowing. There are two reasons for this

- to keep the leverage level down
- to strengthen the balance sheet for financial reporting purposes.

When a company is taken over, the purchase price usually is higher than the value of its net assets. This creates goodwill on acquisition. For example, if Alpha Inc. acquires Beta Limited for $10 million, and the value of Beta's net assets is $6 million, there will be $4 million of goodwill on acquisition. Goodwill must be accounted for in the group accounts of the buying company. In the example above, Alpha must account for the $4 million of goodwill on acquiring Beta.

In the past in some countries, the goodwill could be written off against the consolidated reserves of the group. Generally goodwill is treated as an intangible fixed asset and amortized over its estimated useful life.

Some companies are reluctant to finance acquisitions by borrowing, and prefer to offer either stocks or cash from their existing resources. As a consequence, growth through acquisition is constrained by the company's cash resources, and any acquisition policy is one of measured growth. Such companies may have a policy of accumulating cash resources to enable them to take advantage of any opportunities as and when they arise.

Some companies could use borrowing partially to finance an acquisition, but at the same time try to limit borrowing in order to keep leverage at a tolerable level.

Post Acquisition Refinancing

A problem for the bidding company in a takeover is uncertainty about the number of offer acceptances from the target company stockholders. Without knowing exactly how much finance will be required, it can be difficult to select the most suitable financing structure for the acquisition.

A solution that could be appropriate in this situation would be to make a cash offer, financed by short-term borrowings, a debt bridge. When the acquisition has been completed, and the exact amount of financing is known, a refinancing arrangement can be put in place by arranging a long-term bank loan or bond issue, and using the money to repay the bridging finance.

Structuring a Merger

Mergers can be fairly complex structures. An agreement is needed about the corporate structure and stockholding structure for the combined enterprise. Arrangements can vary widely, and mergers usually will involve the creation of one or more new companies.

Example 1

BT's proposed merger with MCI in 1997 was, strictly speaking, structured as an acquisition. In this case, BT proposed to acquire all the stocks in MCI and integrate the two businesses in Concert, a new UK-based company. Both BT and MCI would provide a joint chairman for the merged company. BT and MCI stockholders were to be issued with stocks in Concert. Under the original offer, MCI stockholders would have owned 33% of Concert's stocks; under the revised offer they would have owned about 25%.

Example 2

In 1998 the publishing companies, Wolters Kluwer and Reed Elsevier announced a proposed merger. The transaction was to be structured as a stock-swap, with Reed Elsevier exchanging 7.85 stocks in its Dutch partner Elsevier NV for one Wolters Kluwer stock.

Reed Elsevier was jointly owned by the UK's Reed International, and Dutch Elsevier NV. After the merger, Reed stockholders were to own 38.3% of the stocks, Elsevier stockholders 34.2% and Wolters Kluwer stockholders 27.5%.

Subsequently the transaction was called off because of European Union merger regulations.

6

The Regulation of Mergers and Takeovers

Mergers and takeovers, particularly those involving large public companies, are subject to a variety of regulations. These differ between countries, but include regulations

- restricting mergers and takeovers that would create a trust (or monopoly) in the market
- preventing or restricting the acquisition of companies in key industries
- governing the conduct and procedures of takeover bids.

Monopolies and the Public Interest

Many countries have laws governing the creation of monopolies, or business combinations that would be against the public interest. The strict definition of a monopoly is a company that is the only supplier to a particular market. However, for practical purposes, proposed mergers and acquisitions are subject to investigation if they would give the company a dominant position in its market.

A merger or acquisition might be forbidden when it is considered against the public interest by

- reducing competition in the market
- (in all probability) raising prices in the market
- restricting supply outlets
- reducing export competitiveness
- reducing market efficiency.

The US

Strong government action against monopolies dates back to the trust-busting activities of governments early in the 20th century, when giant corporations such as Standard Oil were broken up into a number of smaller businesses.

The most recent government measure was the Hart-Scott-Rodino antitrust legislation, the 1976 Antitrust Improvement Act. Any intention to acquire more than 15% or $15 million of a public company's voting shares must be reported to the Federal Trade Commission, the Antitrust Division of the Department of Justice and the target. Subsequently, the federal government then has 30 days in which to object to the acquisition of the shares.

Several states have enacted their own business combination laws or share control acquisition laws that are intended to make mergers and acquisitions, particularly highly leveraged buyouts, more difficult.

Example
When Texas Utilities Co made a bid for UK-owned Energy Group plc, it was required under state law to obtain regulatory approval from the Public Utility Commission to invest more than 30% of its capital abroad.

Rules in the USA

Takeover activity in the USA is regulated on a federal level under the 1968 Williams Act, that governs the operation of tender offers. Additional, and very varied rules apply to takeovers in individual states.

The UK

In the UK, a proposed merger or acquisition can be referred to the Competitions Commission (CC) for investigation, to assess whether it would be against the public interest. Referrals are made by the government minister responsible, the Secretary of State for the Department of Trade and Industry, at the recommendation of the Office of Fair Trading (OFT). Referrals to the CC could be recommended if

- the acquisition would result in the company having a UK market share of 25% or more
- the value of the acquisition exceeds a certain amount (currently £70 million)
- the acquisition of a newspaper is involved, or the merger of two or more water enterprises.

Negotiations about a possible takeover can break down when a referral to the CC seems likely. A referral to the CC freezes a takeover bid until the commission's investigation is completed. This can create a delay of up to six months or so, during which time commercial conditions could have changed. The UK's takeover regulations therefore allow a bidder to withdraw or revise its bid if such a referral takes place.

UK law provides for a negotiated way of avoiding referral to the CC. The Office of Fair Trading can negotiate undertakings with the parties to the merger or takeover, and obtain an agreement from them to divest parts of the business that are causing competition concerns. This provision is contained in section 147 of the Companies Act 1989 that amended the Fair Trading Act 1973. If a suitable undertaking is given, referral to the CC is not required. It is also possible for companies to consult unofficially with the OFT before announcing a takeover in order to get a reliable indication of whether a referral will be made.

Example
In 1998, Ladbroke acquired the Coral group of betting offices. In an effort to forestall an CC enquiry, it simultaneously agreed the sale of 10% of the outlets. In the event the acquisition was referred to the CC that blocked the deal, obliging Ladbroke to sell the business within six months.

The European Union

Within the European Union, the supervision and regulation of merger activity is the responsibility of the commissioner for competitive policy. In 1989, the individual EU countries granted the European Commission the power to block or veto large mergers and takeovers.

Some powers had already been granted to the EU by the Treaty of Rome (Article 85 on cartels and Article 86 on monopolies). In the mid-1980s the commission had used its influence to challenge the terms of the purchase of the Rover Group by British Aerospace and to prevent the acquisition of Irish Distillers by a consortium of Grand Metropolitan, Allied-Lyons and Guinness.

Under EU merger regulations, the commission has the exclusive right to investigate cross-border mergers above a certain threshold value with a community dimension. The threshold limit is subject to periodic review. Currently the thresholds are

- all merging parties having combined worldwide aggregate turnover of at least euro 2.5 billion
- at least two of the parties having aggregate EU-wide turnover of more than euro 100 million
- all merging companies having combined turnover of more than euro 100 million in each of at least three EU states
- in each of the three EU states, each of at least two of the merging parties having turnover of more than euro 25 million.

If each threshold is reached, the merger is referred to the European Commission that has sole jurisdiction. For companies involved in cross-border mergers and takeovers, this has the advantage of one-stop approval, because a proposed deal would have to be referred to just one body instead of several bodies in each of the countries affected. The commission has the power to refer a decision to a member state.

National governments, on the other hand, have been somewhat reluctant to cede powers to the EU, and have sought to retain their own authority.

Example
In 1997 Lafarge of France made a bid for Redland of the UK. The bid was referred to the European Commission that in turn referred part of

the bid – the question of whether there was a potential monopoly in Redland's UK markets – to the UK Competitions Commission in early 1998.

Other Countries

Similar bodies in many other countries enforce anti-monopoly legislation. In Japan the regulation and supervision of mergers and takeovers, and enforcement of antitrust laws, is the responsibility of the Fair Trade Commission. It can block mergers and takeovers, or insist that certain conditions be met, for example, that a bidder divest part of its own businesses or the target company's business.

Specific Industry Restrictions

In many countries, the government retains the right to block takeovers in key industries where a change of ownership could be against the public interest. Key industries generally include the media, defense and communications. Control can be exercised by the granting of operating licenses to approved market participants. Refusing to grant a license to the new owner can block takeovers.

Example
Until 1996 the US telecommunications industry was highly regulated. Following the break-up of the original AT&T in 1982 into seven Baby Bell operators with local monopolies, came federal restrictions on mergers and the exclusion of the Baby Bells from long distance services. However the deregulation of the industry in 1996 was closely followed by the merger of, first, SBC Communications and Pacific Telesis, and second, Bell Atlantic and Nynex, the first two transactions in a new wave of acquisition activity.

Rules Governing Conduct and Procedures

Stock exchange authorities can establish rules of conduct for parties involved in a takeover or merger that apply to companies whose shares are listed on the exchange. The main purpose of these rules is to make sure that the interests of the shareholders of both companies in a bid (buyer and seller) are properly protected. The regulations are directed chiefly at the conduct of the buying company's directors (or shareholders) and the selling company's directors and their advisers. Rules of conduct, like other regulations, differ between countries.

Hostile Bids and Defense Tactics

A distinction can be made between acquisitions that are

- aggressive
- defensive
- negotiated.

In an aggressive or hostile takeover bid, the buyer tries to acquire the target company in the face of strong opposition from the target company's board of directors. Both sides put their conflicting views to the target company's stockholders who, individually, can accept or reject the offer for their shares.

A defensive acquisition is a response to a hostile takeover bid. A company's directors, faced with a hostile bid that might succeed, could try to persuade a more suitable friendly company (a white knight) to put in an alternative bid. They would then recommend to their stockholders this alternative offer.

In a negotiated acquisition, the bidder and the target company's management negotiate on price, purchase consideration (cash or shares, etc.) and other terms of purchase. An agreed deal is worked out and recommended to the target company's stockholders by the management.

There are crucial differences between a hostile bid and a negotiated bid. The target company's stockholders are encouraged by their board of directors to refuse a hostile bid. The chances of a successful bid therefore are lower than with a negotiated bid.

In a hostile bid, the target company is unwilling to provide the bidder with any information about its trading position, revenues, costs, profits, management systems, etc. In a negotiated bid, the target company will be prepared to release some information to the bidder, subject to the signing of a confidentiality agreement. This helps the bidder to fix an offer price.

In a negotiated bid, the target company normally will be willing to give certain warranties and indemnities to the buyer. In a hostile bid, there are no warranties or indemnities from the target company.

In many cases, a potential buyer will not contemplate a hostile bid, and will not proceed with an offer if the target company's management say the company is not for sale.

Frequency of Hostile Bids

Hostile takeover bids were fairly common in the US and UK during the mid 1980s, when relatively easy access to debt financing allowed companies to make leveraged takeover deals. In the early 1990s the economic recession and the financial difficulties of many companies that had over-borrowed made hostile bids less likely because it was more difficult to raise the cash that a hostile bid would usually require, to buy out the target company shareholders. Investors and financiers are likely to be concerned about the economic arguments in favor of the takeover, and the possibility that the bidding company could suffer a dilution in earnings per share, or get into some form of financial difficulty through over-borrowing.

Some hostile bids are very large, for example, the 1997 bidding battle for MCI Communications discussed earlier, where GTE bid the highest price of $33.51 billion for the company. The number of large cross-border hostile bids has also increased, for example, the £1.1 billion Hercules bid for Allied Colloids in 1997.

Defensive Strategy

Defending a company against takeover bids often requires a

- long-term strategy, to discourage any potential bidders, and
- a short-term tactic, to resist a specific bid.

Perhaps the most effective long-term defensive strategy is to achieve continuing growth in profits and dividends, and a high share price. If a company is successful, its management should have the support of its major institutional investors. A track record of rising dividends and share price should create confidence in the future. A hostile bid would then have to be at a very high price to stand a chance of succeeding. A potential bidder, without access to more detailed figures about the target company's performance that could be supplied in a friendly bid will be uncertain about how much to offer. If a target company's directors indicate their hostility to a possible bid, the potential bidder often will give up the attempt immediately.

On the assumption that a good offense is the best defense, a company could protect itself from takeover bids by pursuing an acquisition strategy of its own.

Some companies protect themselves against hostile bids through cross-border strategic alliances, in the form of cross-shareholdings. One company can issue shares to another, receiving shares in the other company in return. For example, a UK company and a French company could agree to exchange shares in each other, amounting to perhaps 20% of the voting shares. In the event of a hostile takeover bid for either company, the board of directors of the target company could then count on the certain support of 20% of their shareholders in rejecting the bid.

Defense Tactics

When a hostile takeover bid is received, the board of directors must organize defense tactics. Such tactics can vary between countries depending on what is permissible by law or under stock market regulations. In all cases, however, the directors should begin by assessing the value of their company, and consider why they believe the offer price to be unacceptable.

Defense by Argument

The most appropriate and common way of resisting a takeover bid is to use the force of argument. A defense document can be issued to stockholders explaining why, in the opinion of the board of directors, shareholders should not accept the offer.

Various arguments against a takeover can be used. They should all lead to a conclusion that the bid is too low and undervalues the shares. Possible arguments are that

- future profits of the company (earnings per share) will be strong, and the offer price fails to reflect this. A profit forecast can be provided.
- future business prospects of the company are good, and it should prosper without a takeover
- (if the bidder were offering a share-for-share swap) the prospects of the company after an acquisition would be much worse than if the company remained independent
- the dividends per share are high, and the present offer price fails to reflect this
- the company will pay an increased dividend if there is no takeover
- the company's assets have a high value that is not reflected in the offer price
- the directors have an alternative strategy for releasing shareholder value, for example a demerger, or sales of selected businesses.

White Knight Defense

In a white knight defense, a target company's board of directors persuades another company (a white knight) to make a rival but friendly bid. The rival bid can be circulated to shareholders, accompanied by a statement of support from the company's directors.

To be successful, however, the price offered by the rival bidder must be sufficiently attractive to win shareholder support.

Poison Pill Defense

A poison pill is a measure that will be implemented if an unfriendly takeover bid occurs, making the takeover less attractive to the bidder.

The term poison pill can be used to mean anything that could deter a hostile bid. In its proper meaning, however, poison pills referred to measures that would alter the voting rights of existing stockholders in the event of a hostile bid. This type of poison pill is prohibited in the UK by company law, but can be used in other countries.

Changing the voting rights of stockholders to protect the company against a takeover bid has been used by Dutch company Philips and by French companies Compagnie Générale d'Electricité and Lafarge Coppée.

Over 60% of US companies in the S&P 500 have poison pill defenses, most dating from the mid-to-late 1980s, and subject to review after ten years. Institutional stockholder pressure has forced some boards of directors to resubmit them for shareholder approval. The concern of shareholders should be that a poison pill defense, by discouraging takeover bids, might be against their interests. A few US companies, such as Kmart, the retail group, and Philip Morris in 1995, have dropped their poison pill defense as a result of stockholder pressure. Prior to its merger with Daimler-Benz, Chrysler renewed its poison pill in 1996 but altered the terms to become more middle of the road. Its poison pill now would not be triggered if the group receives a fully financed all-cash bid deemed to be at a fair price by an independent investment bank.

In the US (unlike Canada or the UK) a company's board of directors without stockholder approval can introduce poison pills.

There are several types of poison pill. These include

- super-voting rights that give existing stockholders the right to apply for preferred stock that give special voting rights. This can make it more difficult for a bidder to gain control of the company
- giving existing stockholders the right to subscribe for new shares in their company at a deep discount in the event of a buyer acquiring a substantial shareholding.

The aim of a poison pill is to

- restrict the voting rights of unwanted bidders who acquire shares in the company, or
- dilute the shareholding of an unwanted bidder by offering new lower priced shares to the other shareholders.

Example

In late 1997 the Italian luxury goods group Gucci attempted to introduce voting restrictions on its shares. The restrictions would have prevented an investor from controlling more than 20% of the voting rights, no matter how many shares were owned. Although this was not described as a poison pill, it would have had the effect of encouraging a substantial shareholder to make a public offer for all the shares in the company rather than acquire shares on the market in a dawn raid.

A poison pill also can be introduced in the course of a takeover bid to deter a rival bidder, or to compensate the original bidder should a rival bid succeed. For example, part of the merger agreement between BT and MCI in 1997, discussed previously, provided for BT to be paid a $465 million break-up fee if MCI pulled out of its agreement. Further to this, once MCI agreed to the rival bid by WorldCom, so making itself liable for the break-up fee to BT, the two companies agreed to pay each other $750 million if either pulled out of the deal. If the WorldCom-MTI deal failed, BT would be paid a further $250 million and MCI would receive very substantial liquidated damages.

Disposal of Assets

A target company's board of directors could respond to a hostile bid by selling off their most attractive assets to another buyer. This would make the company less attractive to the bidder.

In an extreme case, a company might sell off all its saleable assets when a hostile bid occurs, leaving very little left for the bidder to acquire. This is known as a scorched earth defense. (UK public companies are not permitted such forms of defense.)

Fatman Defense

An alternative to disposing of attractive assets is to acquire unattractive assets. In a fatman defense, a company acquires a large underperforming company, as a means of deterring a hostile bid.

Sketchley Defense

A bidder for a public company generally makes it a condition of the bid that there should have been no material adverse change in the target company since its last financial statements. A target company's board of directors can establish a defense against the bid by stating that the company is in a much worse financial position than its most recent published results indicate. In effect, a Sketchley defense is intended to deter the bidder.

Golden Parachute

The directors and key executives of some companies have contracts of employment that provide for a lump sum payment in the event of a takeover by another company. These payments are known as golden parachutes. The purpose of a golden parachute is to give the directors income protection, should they be dismissed after the takeover.

If payments were to be very large, it could be argued that a golden parachute tempts directors to welcome a takeover bid. These arrangements in directors' employment contracts can be a disincentive to a potential bidder. Golden parachutes add to the overall cost of a takeover without giving the buyer any benefit.

Restrictions on Defense Tactics

Defense tactics can be restricted by local laws or stock market rules.
During the course of an offer, or even earlier if a bid is expected shortly,
a company must obtain the prior consent of its stockholders to

- issue or buy back new shares, convertible securities or share
  warrants
- make material alterations to the terms of directors' contracts
- issue share options
- sell or purchase assets of a material value
- enter into any contracts outside the normal course of business.

Demergers and Divestments

A successful business should grow, and business management in general has a growth culture. However, increasingly in recent years there has been widespread recognition that growth must have a direction. Sometimes it can best serve the objectives of corporate strategy to

- sell parts of the business in order to concentrate resources on core business areas, or
- split the business into completely separate parts to unlock value, and allow each part to develop independently.

Divestments and Core Businesses

Selling divisions to concentrate on core businesses has been a common feature of corporate strategy in recent years. This has created a supply of businesses/subsidiary companies for acquisitive companies to buy in negotiated takeovers.

Example
In 1998 Tomkins plc, the US/UK conglomerate, sold its fastener distribution businesses in the UK and Europe and its US fruit retail operation. This move came shortly after the announcement of Tomkins' acquisition of the Spillers flour milling business, to add to its existing RHM flour business. The transactions were in line with Tomkins' strategy of focusing on its manufacturing activities, moving away from distribution and retail.

A decision to divest and concentrate on core businesses sometimes can be prompted by a failed diversification strategy.

Demergers

A divestment involves a company selling off some of its businesses to an external purchaser. A demerger, by contrast, is the splitting of one company into two separate independent companies. The shareholders of the company before the demerger own all or most of the shares in the two companies after demerger.

Demerger

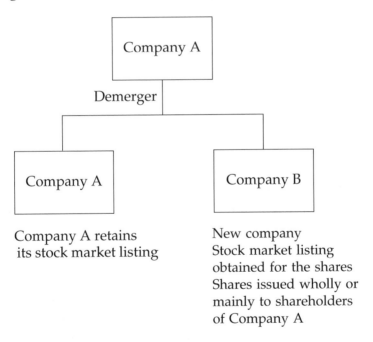

Company A retains
its stock market listing

New company
Stock market listing
obtained for the shares
Shares issued wholly or
mainly to shareholders
of Company A

Reason for Demergers

The principal reason for a demerger is a recognition by a company's management that their operating activities have a broad scope, and that different parts of the business will perform better if they are completely separated. A demerger strategy, in effect, is the direct opposite of a strategy of conglomerate diversification.

A conglomerate can manage separate businesses independently. Shareholders, however, must invest in the shares of the conglomerate as a whole. In contrast, if a company is demerged, shareholders can choose in which part of the previously united company they wish to invest. They can invest separately in both demerged companies if they wish.

By undergoing a demerger, it could be possible to unlock value in the company by obliging stock market investors to value each demerged business separately.

Example
Echo Inc. consists of two separate businesses, hotels and food production. The current annual earnings (after-tax profits) are

	£ million
Hotels	10
Food	<u>40</u>
Total	50

The market value of Echo's shares is $400 million, valuing the company on a price/earnings multiple of eight ($400 million ÷ $50 million).

Echo's directors believe the stock market undervalues the company's shares, arguing that food producing companies are valued on a price/earnings multiple of about eight, while hotels companies are valued on a multiple of about 14.

The directors of Echo decide on a demerger, retaining food production within Echo Inc., and establishing a new company Foxtrot Inc. to operate the hotels business. Shares in Foxtrot are issued to Echo's shareholders and listed on the stock market.

Analysis
If Echo's directors are correct, the demerger should unlock value for their

shareholders. They can sell their shares in Echo or Foxtrot, if they do not want to invest in food production or hotels respectively. The shareholders of both companies therefore could change.

The combined value of the two companies should be higher than the $400 million value of Echo's shares before the demerger.

	Possible market value
	$million
Echo plc ($40 million x 8)	320
Foxtrot plc ($10 million x 14)	140
	460

Examples of demergers aimed at unlocking value and allowing shareholders to invest in specific businesses rather than in a conglomerate group have been fairly common.

Example 1
In January 1998, CPC International, the major US foods group, decoupled its branded foods operation, renamed Bestfoods Inc, from the core corn refining business to reflect the differential between the two businesses. In the year since the demerger was first announced, CPC's share price increased by 32%.

Example 2
Hanson plc, the UK/US conglomerate, was widely regarded as the king of the takeover game of the 1980s. However, in the 1990s it formulated a new strategy of demerging its businesses into four separate entities, each focusing on a particular industry sector. The final move was when its international energy interests were spun off into the newly quoted Energy Group plc in February 1997. This left Hanson with its core business of aggregates and building products. Lord Hanson maintained that in the absence of suitable acquisition targets, the demerger plan was the best means of creating greater management and growth opportunities.

Example 3

ICI, prompted by rumors of a bid from Hanson in 1992, decided to spin off its pharmaceuticals, agrochemicals and specialty chemicals divisions. These were combined into a company, Zeneca, that was floated on the London Stock Exchange in 1993. The strategy behind the demerger was to unlock value for the shareholders, in the belief that the total market value of the demerged companies (Zeneca and ICI) would be higher than the value of ICI before the demerger. This has proved to be the case.

Accounting Issues

Mergers and acquisitions can have a significant effect on a company's profits and net assets. The financial reporting aspects of M&A are therefore important, not least in affecting share values. The accounting rules vary between countries, but in broad terms, the key issues are the same, and are described briefly here.

Merger Accounting and Acquisition Accounting

Merger accounting and acquisition accounting are two different methods of reporting the income and consolidated balance sheet of a business combination. The main difference is that

- in merger accounting, the pre-merger incomes of both companies are brought into reserves in the combined balance sheet, but
- in acquisition accounting, the pre-acquisition income of the acquired company is excluded from reserves in the consolidated balance sheet.

Example
Two companies, Alpha and Beta, decided to combine. The balance sheets of the companies at the date of the merger were

	Alpha	Beta
	$million	$million
Net assets	400	300
Stocks of $1 each	100	100
Retained earnings	300	200
	400	300

Alpha's stocks have a market value of $5. It was agreed that Beta's business should be valued at $400 million. The merger was achieved by means of Alpha issuing 80 million stocks in exchange for Beta's stocks. Alpha therefore has 180 million stocks in issue after the merger, and owns Beta's stocks.

The balance sheet of Alpha, as at the merger date, is

	$million
Net assets at merger date	400
Investment in Beta's stocks, at nominal value	80
	480
Share capital (100 + 80)	180
Retained earnings	300
	480

Because in this case merger accounting is used the investment is recorded at nominal value.

Analysis
The application of merger accounting or acquisition accounting concerns the consolidated results and financial position of the Alpha group.

Merger accounting
In merger accounting the balance sheet includes all the net assets and pre-merger retained earnings of both companies.

Alpha Group (merger accounting)

	$million
Net assets (400 + 300)	700
Share capital (100 + 80)	180
Retained earnings (300 + 200)	500
Other reserve	20
	700

The other reserve occurs because of the difference between the $100 million nominal value of Beta's stocks and the $80 million nominal value of Alpha's stocks, for which they were exchanged.

Acquisition accounting

In acquisition accounting, the pre-merger income of the acquired company cannot be included in the group's financial statements.

Because Alpha has issued stocks to buy Beta's stocks, Alpha has acquired Beta. Beta's pre-acquisition income of $200 million cannot be included in the group balance sheet.

In acquisition accounting, there is an amount of purchased goodwill. Goodwill is the difference between the price paid for an acquisition and the value of the assets acquired. In this example, Alpha issued stocks at an agreed valuation of $400 million to acquire net assets of $300 million. The excess is purchased goodwill of $100 million.

The commonly accepted view is that purchased goodwill should be shown as an asset in the group's balance sheet, and gradually amortized over a period of several years. The amortization would be charged against the profits of the group. This is current practice in the US and now in the UK, where goodwill amortization is tax deductible.

The balance sheet of Alpha at the acquisition date would be

Alpha Group (acquisition accounting)

	$million
Net assets (400 + 300)	<u>700</u>
Share capital	180
Share premium (Alpha)	320
Retained earnings (300 - 100)	<u>200</u>
	700

The retained earnings excludes Beta's pre-merger income. It consists of Alpha's retained earnings of $300 million minus the $100 million of purchased goodwill written off.

If you compare the group balance sheets using merger accounting and acquisition accounting, the attractiveness of merger accounting should be apparent. Retained earnings are higher, in this example $500 million versus $200 million.

In practise, however, the use of merger accounting is restricted. Most international financial reporting of consolidated accounts uses the acquisition method.

Purchased Goodwill

For the purpose of financial reporting, two major areas of concern are

- how to account for purchased goodwill, and
- how to value purchased goodwill.

Accounting for Purchased Goodwill

Subject to local rules, purchased goodwill either can be treated as a fixed asset or written off in full against reserves in the year of acquisition. An example might help to illustrate the implications of each method.

Example

Gamma Inc. has just acquired Delta Inc. in a cash purchase. Gamma's share capital and reserves at the acquisition date were

	$million
Share capital	200
Retained earnings	1,800
	2,000

The net assets of the group at the acquisition date are $1,750 million, excluding goodwill. Purchased goodwill was $250 million.

Analysis
If the purchased goodwill is treated as an asset, the group's balance sheet will be

	$million
Net assets excluding goodwill	1,750
Goodwill	250
	2,000
Financed by:	
Share capital (Gamma only)	200
Reserves (retained earnings)*	1,800
	2,000

*Gamma's reserves only, because the post-acquisition profits of Delta are nil at the acquisition date.

The goodwill must be amortized over a period of time. Suppose Gamma amortizes the goodwill over a five-year period. In each of the five years following the acquisition, a charge for amortization of goodwill will be made against the group's profits. The annual charge will be $50 million ($250 million ÷ 5 years).

By contrast, if goodwill is written off in full against reserves in the year of acquisition, the group's balance sheet at the acquisition date will be

	$million
Net assets	1,750
Financed by:	
Share capital	200
Reserves less goodwill (1,800 - 250)	1,550
	1,750

The reserves are reduced by the amount of goodwill, but there will be no amortization charge against group profits in any year. The group's annual reported earnings therefore will be higher. For this reason, companies often prefer, if permitted, to write off goodwill in full on acquisition to protect their future reported profits.

In most countries, amortization of goodwill is the norm.

The Value of Purchased Goodwill

Purchased goodwill is the difference between the cost of an acquisition and the fair value of the assets acquired. For example, if a company that is taken over has net assets of $400 million and is purchased for $600 million, purchased goodwill should be $200 million.

However, suppose the company reassesses the value of the net assets it has acquired, and decides that their fair value isn't $400 million, but is only $350 million.

Suppose too that the company believes that it will have to undertake rationalization measures in its acquired subsidiary, scrapping some equipment and making some employees redundant. These measures could cost $25 million.

It can be argued that the value of purchased goodwill should be based on the fair value of the assets that should also allow for future rationalization costs. In this example, purchased goodwill would then be much higher than $200 million

	$ million
Purchase cost	600
Provision for future rationalization	25
	625
Fair value of assets acquired	350
Purchased goodwill	275

The purchased goodwill could, if permitted, be written off in full against reserves. This means that the cost of rationalization measures after the acquisition has taken place (up to $25 million) need never be a charge against annual group profits.

Glossary

Acquisition Accounting
Method of accounting for a takeover in which the pre-acquisition profits of the acquired company are excluded from the reported income, and reserves of the group. The difference between the purchase price and the value of the assets acquired is accounted for as purchased goodwill.

Asset Stripping
Acquiring a target company and selling off (stripping out) its most valuable assets.

CC
Competitions Commission: UK antitrust authority.

City Code
City Code on Takeovers and Mergers. A UK code of practice for public companies involved in a takeover or merger, set out in the Blue Book.

Comparables
A series of financial ratios, calculated for companies in a similar line of business. Used for screening acquisition targets and for putting a valuation to a proposed takeover.

Corporate Raider
Investor seeking undervalued companies as acquisitions, in order to buy cheaply and resell at a profit, perhaps by breaking them up and selling the separate businesses to different buyers.

Demerger
Separation of one company or group into two separate and independent companies or groups.

Due Diligence
Exercise carried out by a prospective bidder in a negotiated bid, to confirm the accuracy of the information and assumptions on which the bid is being based.

Earnings Dilution
Reduction in earnings per share. An acquisition can result in either earnings dilution or earnings enhancement (higher earnings per share) for the buying company.

Earnings Multiple
Method of valuation of a target company. The offer price is based on a multiple of the target company's annual earnings. See P/E ratio.

Earn-Out Agreement
Method of agreeing the purchase price for a private company. The owners are paid a minimum price immediately plus one or more subsequent earn-out payments that depend on the annual profits of the purchased business post-acquisition.

Fatman Defense
An alternative to disposing of attractive assets is to acquire unattractive assets. In a fatman defense, a company acquires a large underperforming company, as a means of deterring a hostile bid.

Goodwill
Amount by which value or consideration exceeds a company's book net asset value.

Golden Parachute
Terms in the service contract of a company's director, providing for a substantial severance payment in the event of dismissal after a merger or a takeover.

Hart-Scott-Rodino Act
The 1976 US antitrust legislation.

Indemnity
Undertaking given by the seller to the buyer in the acquisition of an unquoted company, whereby the buyer will be reimbursed for specified unforeseen costs.

Joint Venture
Strategic alliance between two independent companies, often established as a jointly owned company.

Letter of Intent
Letter from a prospective bidder to the management of a target company, indicating an intention to make a bid subject to a satisfactory outcome from due diligence.

Merger Accounting
Method of accounting for a merger in which all the pre-merger profits of both companies are included in the reported profits and reserves of the merged businesses.

Offer Document
Formal letter to the stockholders of a target company, offering to purchase their stocks and asking for acceptance.

Pacman Bid
Defense to a hostile bid, whereby the target makes a counter-bid to acquire the bidder.

Paper Offer
Takeover in which the purchase consideration will be paid in the form of newly issued securities (stocks, etc.) of the buying company.

Partial Acquisition
Acquisition of a controlling interest in a company, normally over 50% of the equity stock.

Payback Period
Time taken for a project to recover its original investment.

P/E Ratio
Ratio used in valuation of a company. A P/E ratio is calculated as price per stock divided by net earnings per stock.

Poison Pill
A measure that may be implemented in the event of a hostile bid to deter the bidder or make it more difficult for the bid to succeed.

This tactic usually involves a change to the voting rights or stockholdings of existing stockholders.

Purchased Goodwill
Difference between the purchase price of an acquisition and the fair value of the assets acquired.

Sketchley Defense
Takeover defense by which target renders itself unattractive to the bidder by presenting itself in an unfavorable light.

Spin-off
Distribution of shares in a subsidiary to the company's shareholders, so that they hold stocks separately in the two firms.

Synergy
The additional benefits including cost savings, higher revenue, etc., of combining the resources of two companies. Described as the
2 + 2 = 5 effect.

Vertical Integration
Acquiring or merging with the business of a major supplier (backward vertical integration) or a major customer (forward vertical integration).

WACC
Weighted average cost of capital, i.e. the average cost to a company of all its sources of finance.

Warranty
An undertaking given by the seller (owner of a company or its directors) to a buyer in a negotiated takeover of a private company.

White Knight
A friendly bidder for a company whose bid is encouraged by the target company to rival a current hostile takeover bid.

Yellow Book
London Stock Exchange Listing Rules, governing inter alia regulations for acquisitions and disposals by UK-listed companies.

Index